WHOSE VOTE COUNTS?

*"New Democracy Forum operates at a level of literacy and
responsibility which is all too rare in our time."*
—John Kenneth Galbraith

Other books in the New Democracy Forum series:

WHOSE VOTE COUNTS?

ROBERT RICHIE AND STEVEN HILL

EDITED BY JOSHUA COHEN AND JOEL ROGERS
FOR *BOSTON REVIEW*

BEACON PRESS
BOSTON

BEACON PRESS
25 Beacon Street
Boston, Massachusetts 02108-2892
www.beacon.org

Beacon Press books are published under the auspices of the
Unitarian Universalist Association of Congregations.

Originally published as *Reflecting All of Us:
The Case for Proportional Representation*

Printed in the United States of America

04 03 02 01   8 7 6 5 4 3 2 1

This book is printed on acid-free paper that meets the uncoated paper
ANSI/NISO specifications for permanence as revised in 1992.

Composition by Wilsted & Taylor Publishing Services

Library of Congress Cataloging-in-Publication Data
Richie, Robert.
     [Reflecting all of us]
     Whose vote counts? / Robert Richie and Steven Hill ; edited by Joshua
Cohen and Joel Rogers for Boston review.
     p.   cm. — (New democracy forum)
     Originally published as: Reflecting all of us : the case for proportional
representation. c1999.
     Includes bibliographical references.
     ISBN 0-8070-4423-7 (pbk.)
     1. Proportional representation—United States.   2. Representative
government and representation—United States.   3. Elections—United
States.   I. Hill, Steven.   II. Cohen, Joshua, 1951–   .   III. Rogers, Joel,
1952–   .   IV. Boston review (Cambridge, Mass.: 1982)   V. Title.
VI. Series.
JF1075.U6 R55 2001
328.73'07347—dc21   2001025432

The pure idea of democracy, according to its definition, is the government of the whole people by the whole people, equally represented. Democracy as commonly conceived and hitherto practiced, is the government of the whole people by a mere majority of the people, exclusively represented. The former is synonymous with the equality of all citizens; the latter, strangely confounded with it, is a government of privilege, in favor of the numerical majority, who alone possess practically any voice in the State. This is the inevitable consequence of the manner in which the votes are now taken, the complete disenfranchisement of minorities.

—JOHN STUART MILL, *Representative Government*

CONTENTS

FOREWORD

LANI GUINIER

The decisive moment in the 2000 presidential election did not take place in the voting booths or in the public tabulation of ballots but in the secret deliberations of the U.S. Supreme Court. What began as judicial overreaching when the results of those deliberations were announced on December 12, 2000, in *Bush v. Gore* should now become a clarion call for major democratic reform. Some legal experts argue that the United States Supreme Court decision, though heavily criticized for handing the election to George W. Bush, could help open the local courthouse doors to election reform. These legal optimists rely on language in that decision in which the Court declared that a state may not "by arbitrary and disparate treatment value one person's vote over another."

Perhaps, given its new rhetoric about valuing votes equally in order to restore citizen confidence in the outcome of elections, the Supreme Court's conservative majority will now look closely at other suits based on the principle of equal protection—others that, like *Bush v. Gore*, challenge disparate treatment of voters in voting procedures. But the more important effect of the Court's intervention, bolstered by its choice of language explicitly valuing no person's vote over another's, would be to launch a citizen's pro-democracy movement.

The one person, one vote language of the Court under Chief Justice Earl Warren—language that the recent decision draws on—did exactly that, inspiring civil rights marchers in the 1960s. Current efforts could focus on creating new federal reforms, like financial assistance to poor counties to upgrade voting equipment and the elimination of all ways of recording votes that fail to give the voter feedback as to how his or her intent is being registered. Also needed are meaningful assistance to semiliterate or non-English-speaking voters, twenty-four-hour polling places, and a national Election Day holiday. Enacting standards for federal elections is consistent with the Voting Rights Act, which has banned literacy tests nationwide as prerequisites for voting. That ban was passed by Congress in 1970 and unanimously upheld by the Supreme Court.

But reforms to equalize voting access, while important, are not enough. The circumstances of this election call for a larger focus on issues of representation and participation. If we are to build a genuine pro-democracy movement in this country, we cannot limit ourselves to butterfly ballots and chads.

Voters must have a more meaningful opportunity to participate in the entire democratic process—and not just on Election Day. In our current system of "winner-

take-all" elections, the candidate with the largest number of votes in a geographic unit (an election district)
goes to Congress. This limits the role of citizen's groups
because the only real contest is between the two major
political parties. Only one of two political options or
opinions can "win." This stifles political debate because
it drives candidates to the middle of the spectrum, where
most of the votes are. But the winner need not recognize
or take into account legitimate, dissenting views of those
in the minority. Essentially, whoever wins the most votes
gets all the power.

Moreover, in a winner-take-all system of geographic
districts, representatives choose their voters by estab-
lishing electoral districts. Candidates are reelected not
because they mobilize supporters to go to the polls but
because they use the power of incumbency to draw
the election district lines around those supporters. Too
often, the election takes place when the districts are
drawn, not when the voters go to the polls. Voters' per-
ception, that their votes don't count, is unfortunately
accurate.

In the United States, winner-take-all districts also
tend to dilute minority voting strength. Minority vote
dilution occurs when black or Latino voters can never
elect a candidate of their choice because the majority
electorate is hostile and votes as a racial bloc.

As Robert Richie and Steven Hill argue in the essay
that provoked this forum, we can do better. Democracies

formed more recently than our own—indeed the vast majority of the world's longstanding democracies—have developed more nuanced systems, most adopting some form of proportional representation (PR). In 1994, in the negotiated transition to democracy in South Africa, the leadership rejected winner-take-all elections in favor of proportional voting that would enable the white minority there to have some representation in the legislature. As a result of the negotiated transition, South Africa uses a party list system. Voters vote for a political party. The party fields a list of potential candidates. Not all of the party's candidates will win, unless the party gets 100 percent of the total number of votes cast. The candidates on the party list are only elected in direct proportion to the number of votes cast for the party they represent.

Another PR option is cumulative voting. Cumulative voting allows voting city- or countywide, with each voter in the city or county getting the same number of votes as there are seats up for election. Chilton County, a very rural county in central Alabama with 11 percent black population, adopted cumulative voting in response to a lawsuit brought by black residents. After a federal court found that voting was racially polarized, the county decided to implement cumulative voting to settle the lawsuit. As a result, groups that previously had not been represented—blacks, Republicans, and women—have been elected in significant numbers to both the county commission and the board of education.

Such alternatives to winner-take-all have the potential to encourage voter turnout and more diverse constituencies. They also respond to those, including the current Supreme Court majority, who criticize majority-minority districts for making stereotyped assumptions about minority political views and interests based on racial identity alone. PR systems can strengthen the role of diverse minorities without dividing the electorate along racial lines or along lines of winners and losers. Voters are not coerced into voting based on race or any other affiliation simply because of where they live or what they look like. They are free to form their own constituencies and choose candidates who best represent their interests and values. They can forge multiracial coalitions; indeed, local grassroots organizations might finally have sufficient incentives to do just that, since they would be rewarded politically based on the number of people who actually turned out to vote.

PR is, of course, not a cure-all. We need to consider a wide range of democracy reforms to promote a more *people-based* vision of democracy: conducting simultaneous national and local elections; eliminating runoff elections (which contribute to voter fatigue); allowing weekend voting and extended voting periods; voting by mail; campaign finance reform; reinforcing the obligation of television broadcasters as public trustees to grant free air time to all viable candidates and political parties;

and strengthening political parties and encouraging new ones through PR.

After all, what America needs is a system that disperses power more broadly. Ultimately, proportional and semiproportional systems reflect ideas of cooperation and rotation—the importance of public access to power. Constructive reforms would help to undermine the culture of negative campaigning and candidate-centered politics. Such reforms might also encourage more voter participation and citizen involvement by enabling organized citizens' groups to gain political power commensurate with their effort.

Election reform, including PR, is not, however, primarily about electoral rules. It is not simply about getting more people of color and women into office, although that would be an important incidental benefit. It is about transforming how power itself is exercised and shared. It is about opening up a different kind of political conversation, as elections become forums for voters to express their ideas and choose their representatives. It is about giving citizens their due.

Right now, even active citizens hold a very weak hand. But support for reforms that draw people together in relationships can lead to real change. Many others have learned the same lesson: We cannot rely on change being initiated by those already in power or by those whose dominant operating strategy is public silence and private access. After all, democracy takes place when the silent find their voice, and when we begin to listen to what they have to say.

I hope that this New Democracy Forum on proportional representation initiates a process of speaking and listening on this essential issue of democratic thought and practice.

EDITORS' PREFACE

JOSHUA COHEN AND JOEL ROGERS

The purpose of The New Democracy Forum is to foster honest, serious discussion of pressing national problems, and constructive debate about political solutions. The limits of American democracy is an especially large problem. And, if lead authors Robert Richie and Steven Hill are right, proportional representation (PR) promises to relieve those limits.

To see how, let's start with fundamentals. In Athenian democracy, citizens assembled together to make the laws. In American democracy, we elect representatives who make the laws. Virtually all such elections are decided on "winner-take-all" rules, in single-member districts. So the candidate who wins the most votes in a district wins office. Other candidates simply lose, and citizens who vote for losers are, arguably, left unrepresented by government.

But democracy is supposed to be government by *all the people*, not just a *plurality* or *majority* of them. How, then, can we ensure that our government is more inclusive of minority groups and currents of opinion that cannot now win pluralities or majorities? How, in short, can we make government more fully democratic?

An increasingly prominent answer is that the United States should shift to PR. The idea behind PR is that the distribution of representatives in the legislature matches the distribution of votes in the population: if 60 percent of voters support a party, that party wins 60 percent of the legislative seats; if 10 percent support a small party, that party wins 10 percent of the seats. Everyone gets represented, and government becomes more democratic.

That's the basic argument for PR. Robert Richie and Steven Hill develop it here with great clarity and force. They were the obvious choices to write the lead article for this Forum. Richie and Hill are the leading national proponents of PR, and their own work—as writers, speakers, and campaign consultants—powerfully exemplifies the marriage of analysis and political engagement that we aspire to in the New Democracy Forum.

In making the case for PR, Richie and Hill add much to the basic argument. They claim that it would increase voter turnout by encouraging political competition; produce a smarter, more functional democracy by sharpening political debate and making electoral outcomes depend less on the fluctuating sensibilities of "swing voters"; and correct gender and racial imbalances in representation. These are large constitutional and political claims, with substantial implications for political mobilization. To test them, we invited response from a distinguished and diverse group of lawyers, political scientists, elected representatives, and activists. Some of the respondents worry about "governability" under PR. They fear that PR will multiply political parties, thus making collective decisions even harder to achieve than they already are. Others fear that the increase in district size implied by a shift away from single-member districts would drive up the already-exorbitant costs of campaigns, undercutting the weaker candidates or parties Richie and Hill seek to include. And several contributors wonder about feasibility: how can a reform of political process excite the energies needed to overcome an alliance of hostile opposition and sheer inertia?

Despite these reservations, none of the respondents asks "why bother?" They share Richie and Hill's doubts about the fairness and functionality of the current rules of American political competition. And they agree, too, that this large problem in American democracy commands our collective attention. Let the debate begin.

1

THE CASE FOR PROPORTIONAL REPRESENTATION

ROBERT RICHIE AND STEVEN HILL

Nearly all elections in the United States are based on the winner-take-all principle: voters for the candidate who gets the most votes win representation; voters for the other candidates win nothing. This system is unjust and unnecessary. It is unjust because it leaves minorities (whether racial or political) unrepresented. As John Stuart Mill said, "It is an essential part of democracy that minorities should be adequately represented. No real democracy, nothing but a false show of democracy, is possible without it."[1] It is unnecessary because we have immediate opportunities, at local, state, and national levels, to join the vast majority of mature democracies that have already adopted systems of proportional representation.

Proportional representation (PR) is based on the principle that any group of like-minded voters should win legislative seats in proportion to its share of the popular vote. Whereas the winner-take-all principle awards 100 percent of the representation to a 50.1 percent majority,

PR allows voters in a minority to win their fair share of representation.

How does this work? A typical winner-take-all system divides voters into "one-seat districts," represented by one person. With PR, voters in a constituency instead have several representatives: ten one-seat districts might, for example, be combined into a single ten-seat district. A party or group of voters that wins 10 percent of the popular vote in this district, then, would win one of the ten seats; a party or slate of candidates with 30 percent of votes would win three seats, and so forth. Various mechanisms work to provide proportional representation, and the details of different systems matter. But the principle of full representation is fundamental. Acceptance of it changes the way one sees electoral politics.

WHAT'S THE PROBLEM?

Consider three current failures of our winner-take-all system of representation:

- Members of racial and ethnic minorities are under-represented;
- Voters' choices are restricted to candidates within the two-party, Republican/Democratic monopoly;
- Most legislative elections are effectively "no-choice" contests in districts dominated by a single party.

By restricting voters' choices and underrepresenting voters from minority groups, winner-take-all elections devalue the right to vote, our fundamental democratic right. Correcting these failures requires PR. No other political reform currently on the table—public financing of elections, term limits, fusion, or universal voter registration—will suffice to correct these deficiencies in our democracy.

Representation of Racial Minorities

At every level of government, the proportion of black, Latino, and Asian-American elected officials lags far behind these groups' share of the electorate. When members of a racial or ethnic group make up a majority of the electorate in a winner-take-all election, they tend to elect a member of their racial or ethnic group. Every majority-black U.S. House district has a black representative; and in the 49 white-majority states, 144 of 147 U.S. senators and governors are white (as we write, in September 1998). Most racial minorities clearly prefer representatives of their race, but winner-take-all elections often deny them a realistic opportunity to elect candidates of their choice. A quarter of our population is black or Latino, but these groups are in the minority in every state and as a consequence hold only one of 100 U.S. Senate seats. The fact of such underrepresentation throughout our legislatures undercuts their legitimacy and effectiveness in addressing issues of concern to racial and ethnic minorities.

Two Parties

Winner-take-all elections prop up our two-party monopoly. Since 1960, new parties have formed at comparable rates in the United States and in European democracies using PR. But new parties in the United States are almost completely shut out of representation, whereas half the new parties in the European systems eventually have won seats—and the influence and organizing ability that comes from electoral viability.[2] Polls show most Americans would like to see a third party electing candidates at every level of government, but only three of our nearly eight thousand state and congressional legislators were elected on a minor-party ticket—all of them in Burlington, Vermont.

Minor parties by definition begin with minority support, which wins nothing in winner-take-all elections unless it is geographically concentrated. With little chance to win, minority party candidates cannot build or sustain support. Ross Perot's well-financed independent candidacy in 1992 won 19 percent of the vote, but he did not finish first in any congressional district. In 1996, his vote was reduced by more than half, although one voter in ten still voted for minor-party presidential candidates, and half of all eligible voters saw no reason to participate.

"No-Choice" Elections

One-party dominance of most American legislative districts provides a more subtle, but more sweeping, indictment of our winner-take-all system. Most Americans, most of the time, experience "no-choice" elections for city council, state legislature, and the U.S. House of Representatives. In the last ten House elections, for example, more than 90 percent of incumbents were reelected. The average margin of victory in House races is consistently over 30 percent. More than one-third of state legislative races in the 1990s were not even nominally contested by both major parties; fully 68 percent were not contested in Massachusetts in 1996. So-called "swing" legislative districts feature genuine competition and a chance for voters to cast a meaningful vote, but they are exceptions.

The dominance of one-party districts should be no surprise: gerrymandering allows legislators to choose their constituents in redistricting before their constituents go to the polls to choose representatives. Even though political intentions can be removed from the redistricting process—as in Iowa's criteria-driven procedure, for example—its political effects are unavoidable. Given that some (perhaps most) districts will be noncompetitive in winner-take-all elections, all districting ends up as some form of gerrymandering.

The ramifications of our fundamentally lopsided political landscape are often ignored in debates over term limit proposals and campaign finance reform. The real culprit for noncompetitive elections is winner-take-all elections, not incumbency and inequities in campaign spending. In most districts, a clear majority of voters prefers one party's political philosophy to that of the other party. Consider open-seat elections, with no incumbent competing for the seat, and none of the financial advantages that come with incumbency. In 1996, Republicans won 29 of 35 open House seats in districts where Bill Clinton ran behind his national average, despite being outspent in a third of their victories. Yet Republicans won none of the 18 districts where Clinton ran ahead of his national average, despite being financially competitive in half of those defeats. This trend is not confined to elections in presidential years. Overall, Democrats hold 99 of the 100 U.S. House districts where Clinton ran most strongly in 1996. Of the 150 districts where he ran most weakly, Republicans hold 134.

To be sure, congressional winners usually outspend their opponents. But that is because money follows power: to gain access, most major campaign contributors invest in candidates they expect to win. The great majority of voters are consistent in their voting patterns both between and within elections. We should be relieved that voters are well-grounded in a political philosophy, but frustrated that this consistency leads to most of them experiencing no-choice elections.[3]

WHY PR?

Support for PR as an alternative to winner-take-all politics has come from a diverse and distinguished group, including Alexis de Tocqueville, Charles Beard, Walter Lippman, Jane Addams, A. Philip Randolph, Robert Kennedy, and, quietly, Franklin Roosevelt. The most outspoken early supporter of PR was John Stuart Mill, in his *Representative Government* (1861)—written less than two decades after the first works detailing possible PR systems.

The Majoritarian Argument

Perhaps Mill's most important contribution to the case for PR was his argument that majority rule itself is improved by full minority representation. By maximizing the number of voters who elect candidates, he pointed out, PR increases the chances that a legislative majority has support from a majority of voters; it is required for full representation, with voters having the power to elect representatives reflecting a range of opinion; and it fosters a deliberative legislative process which improves the majority view by ensuring that minority opinions are represented and heard.

As Mill observed, any particular majority is a collection of minorities, not a monolithic bloc. Once some voters are excluded from representation, policy can be

{ 9 }

passed without the support of a majority of the electorate. Suppose, for example, that all representatives win their elections with only 50.1 percent of votes. A law passed with support from only 50.1 percent of the legislators then would have backing from only a quarter of votes cast. Mill's point is no mere theoretical concern. In the 1994 "Republican revolution," in which Democrats lost their 40-year stranglehold on the U.S. House of Representatives, fewer than one in four eligible voters voted for a winning House candidate. As a result, House passage of any particular bill in 1995 required the votes of representatives elected by only 13 percent of eligible voters.

By contrast, legislation in democracies with PR generally requires the support of representatives elected by a far higher percentage of the electorate. In Germany's 1994 elections with PR—with a high turnout and a high percentage of effective votes typical of European PR elections—more than three in four eligible voters elected candidates. (Four in five eligible Germans participated, and 19 in 20 voters elected a representative.) So passage of a bill required the votes of representatives elected by nearly 40 percent of eligible voters.

Majority rule also is undercut by winner-take-all elections because they drive voters into two camps. But two-choice elections obscure shades of difference and create the illusion of majority support for the winner. Mill stressed the importance of voters having a full range of choices and representation of their different communities of interest. "I cannot see," he wrote, "why the feelings and interests which arrange mankind according to localities, should be the only ones thought worthy of being represented." The notion that geography should be the primary basis of representation is even more antiquated now, given the increased mobility of our population, ease of communication across distances, and importance of economic, social, and political associations without geographic definition.

Finally, PR is important for majority interests because, as Mill argued, it provides represented minorities with a platform to challenge conventional wisdom. An advocate of universal suffrage, Mill still was sympathetic to conservative concerns about educated minorities being outvoted by newly enfranchised, less-educated voters. Assuring a voice to the minority eliminated his fears because of his faith in the results of a fully democratic process, with open and organized discussion among competing political ideas and projects. By allowing dissenters to win representation, PR fosters ongoing challenges to majority opinion, and thus complements our First Amendment freedoms.

In conjunction with attack ads, polling, and focus groups, the system of winner-take-all elections has made it extremely difficult to have reasoned political debate on certain contentious issues. These issues can assume great symbolic weight for swing voters—ironically, because they are among the relatively few voters with so little political grounding that they will support either party. The death penalty, for example, has come to represent "toughness" on crime. Because winner-take-all elections make nuanced positions difficult, and require that candidates win the support of politically indifferent swing voters, opponents of the death penalty find it hard to run credible campaigns for president or for most legislative offices. On a whole range of issues—from drug policy to abortion rights to welfare reform—debate in political campaigns tends to be highly stylized, making it that much more difficult to challenge public opinion.

Mill's majoritarian argument for PR gains empirical support from a recent statistical comparison of 12 democracies in Europe.[4] John Huber and G. Bingham Powell contrast a "Proportionate Influence Vision" of democracy, in which "elections are designed to produce legislatures that reflect the preferences of all citizens," with the "Majority Control Vision," in which "democratic elections are designed to create strong, single-party majority governments that are essentially unconstrained by other parties in the policy-making process." They conclude that "governments in the Proportionate Influence systems are on average significantly closer to their median voter than are governments in the Majority Control and Mixed systems. . . . If voters are presented with a wide range of choices and electoral outcomes are proportional, governments tend to be closer to the median."

In short, governance is more likely to take place at the

center of the political spectrum with PR, since the electorate is fully represented and voters are able to express a wider range of preferences. At the same time, fair representation of the margins provides a mechanism to transform policy by shifting the political center. Opposition voices will be heard, and their ideas will be far more likely to be debated. If those ideas win growing support, the major parties will adjust accordingly in order to hold onto their supporters.

Other Reasons for PR

Mill's majoritarian argument is not the only case for PR. Four other claims are commonly offered in its support:

1. PR increases voter turnout. Voter turnout is generally estimated to be 10 to 12 percent higher in nations with PR than in similar nations using winner-take-all elections.[5] This difference is understandable. In the United States, as we indicated, relatively few legislative elections are competitive, and our analysis of recent House elections demonstrates a strong correlation between the degree of competition and the level of participation.[6] People in noncompetitive districts—whether supportive of the majority or minority—might better invest their time and resources by supporting candidates in competitive races elsewhere than by voting in their own.

In PR systems, winning fair representation is dependent on voter turnout. Because nearly every vote will help a party win more seats, voters have more incentive to participate, and parties have incentives to mobilize their supporters. Moreover, parties and other electoral organizations have strong incentives to keep their supporters informed, and informed citizens are more likely to vote.

2. PR provides better representation for racial minorities. The 1982 amendments to the Voting Rights Act resulted in more districts drawn with majorities of racial and ethnic minorities. This increase in "majority-minority districts" produced a remarkable leap in representation of people of color in the U.S. House in 1992. Between 1990 and 1992, the number of black and Latino House members jumped from 35 to 55.

In a series of recent rulings against so-called "racial gerrymandering," the Supreme Court has made it much harder to establish majority-minority districts; the result is almost certain to be a decrease in the number of elected black legislators. Lani Guinier, Jesse Jackson, and other civil rights leaders have argued for PR as an alternative, and already more than 75 localities have adopted semi-proportional systems to settle voting rights cases.[7] By building from a fundamental principle of political fairness, PR could secure voting rights of racial minorities, without specifically targeting minority voters (just as Social Security protects low-income seniors by providing benefits for all).

{ 14 }

In addition to winning a fair share of seats, minorities would have greater opportunities to negotiate for influence because they could "swing" among parties. South Africa used PR in its first all-race elections in 1994, and the two leading parties—the African National Congress and the National Party—ran multiracial slates with messages of inclusion. When New Zealand had its first PR election in 1996, the first Asian citizen was elected, and Pacific Islanders and indigenous Maoris tripled their representation. A Maori-backed party formed a coalition government with the governing party—a party whose relationship with Maoris had been analogous to Republicans' post-1960 relationship with American blacks.

By improving representation, PR in turn encourages minority communities to mobilize and win access to power. From 1925 to 1955, Cincinnati used the "choice voting" form of PR to elect a nine-seat city council. (See appendix for an explanation of choice voting.) In 1929, when blacks were barely 10 percent of the population, a black independent candidate ran a strong campaign. In the next election, he was added to the Republican party's slate and was elected. In 1947, when blacks were 15 percent of the population, a former president of the Cincinnati NAACP ran in large part to defend the choice voting system that was under attack from Republicans seeking to restore their old domination of the council. In an indication that any substantial group of voters cannot be ignored with PR, the other major party slate supported him in 1949. He was elected, resulting in black representatives holding two of nine seats.[8]

3. PR increases the number of women in office. The percentage of women elected to office in the United States—only 11 percent of the U.S. Congress—is scandalously low, particularly in light of the relative strength of the American women's movement compared to other nations with far higher percentages of women legislators. Studies show that women representatives make a qualitative and quantitative difference in the type of legislation introduced and passed, yet the growth of women in state legislatures and Congress has stalled since 1992 despite relatively high turnover and the historic high in women's candidacies in 1996.

In state legislative elections, women win seats in significantly higher percentages in multiseat districts than in one-seat districts.[9] The major reasons for this difference are that women are more likely to run and voters are more likely to seek gender balance when there is more than one seat to fill. Because PR expands options, PR systems give women additional leverage to force the major parties to support more women candidates. In 1994, a threat by women supporters of the major parties in Sweden to form a new women's party led to women winning 41 percent of seats in 1994 because the major parties recruited more women candidates. New Zealand, Italy, and Germany are among a growing number of democracies that use systems with a mix of winner-take-all districts and PR seats.[10] It is instructive that women in all three countries are three times more likely to win seats elected by PR than to win in one-seat districts.

4. PR ends gerrymandering. Drawing district lines for political purposes has occurred from the first redistricting: the term "gerrymander" refers to a Massachusetts district plan drawn in 1812. But gerrymandering has become far more potent in an era of powerful computers, more detailed census information, and better techniques for measuring voter preferences.

As one example, Democrats in control of the redistricting process in Texas in 1991 placed the eight Republican incumbents in districts that were packed to be among the most conservative in the nation. These incumbents were easily reelected in 1992, but Democrats won 21 of the remaining 22 seats with only 50 percent of the statewide vote. Only one race was won by less than 10 percent, and the three open seats went to state legislators serving on redistricting committees. Congresswoman Eddie Bernice Johnson, the primary architect of the plan, admitted in 1997 that the redistricting process "is not one of kindness. It is not one of sharing. It is a power grab."

PR makes gerrymandering of any sort far more difficult. The smaller the percentage of votes that can be "wasted" on losing candidates—49 percent in a winner-take-all race, but less than 20 percent in a five-seat PR election and less than 10 percent in a 10-seat PR election—the harder it is for legislators to manipulate electoral outcomes.

PROGRESSIVES NEED MULTIPARTY POLITICS

The case for PR is fundamentally nonpartisan. Voters across the spectrum can support greater democracy or feel poorly represented by winner-take-all elections. But American political progressives have a particularly urgent need to support PR because of the growing problems created by the lack of a serious electoral vehicle to the Democrats' left. Many progressives overrate their current degree of support in the electorate, while others leap in equal error to desperate conclusions about the electorate's likely conservatism. The more complicated reality is disguised by winner-take-all elections, which divide voters into two camps and leave much progressive thought on the margins of political dialogue and influence.

A progressive party that won 5 to 10 percent of legislative seats in PR elections could have a great impact on public discourse, cross-issue organizing, and the policies of the Democratic Party. Electorally, this party could check the Democrats' rightward drift. It would give the base of the Democratic Party—labor, African-Americans, feminists, environmentalists, defenders of civil liberties—a credible alternative, and thus an influence within the Democratic Party similar to that now held by the relatively few "swing" Democrats willing to vote for Republicans. When all voters, not just the centrist fringe, can swing their votes, the major parties must pay more attention to their base.

In addition, a progressive party would provide an opportunity for progressive activists to join together to build an infrastructure of independent politics—work that is very difficult to pursue in a two-party system that pushes activists into single-issue politics.[11] It would give progressives greater access to media and an ongoing means to challenge conventional wisdom. It is one thing for the media to ignore activists who have no strong supporters in Congress; it would be more difficult to ignore a congressional contingent that consistently demonstrated a credible level of national support.

A progressive party would force healthy, if difficult, policy debates among progressives. Winning 10 percent of the vote in a PR system is hard work. The German Greens have never reached 10 percent nationally, yet have had a remarkable impact on German policy and the environmental positions of both major parties. They are partners in governing coalitions in several German states and may soon be part of the national government. At the same time, Greens have made great strides in building coalitions among their members. Organizing a party need not replace other grassroots organizing: a study of German Greens found that over 80 percent of members were active with an organization outside the Greens. But having the Green Party as a unifying electoral presence has made their other work more effective. American progressives urgently need PR to create a similar unifying electoral vehicle.

With PR, a progressive party also could find unexpected allies. Progressives might not outdo conservatives in winning over the majority. But a winner-take-all, two-party system facilitates "divide-and-conquer" strategies in which a conservative party can cut into the potential economically progressive majority with such wedge social issues as gun control, gay rights, affirmative action, and abortion.

In a two-party system, conservatives can create an electoral majority with a set of positions that can be opposed by the majority of voters, but bring together fervent minorities willing to accept positions they oppose in exchange for support for their issue: social liberals seeking low taxes, blue-collar Catholics opposing abortion, labor union members opposing gun control, and so on. With electable choices across the spectrum, a multiparty system based on PR would allow us to find out where the American people really stand—and on many issues, they arguably will stand to the left of current policy. The political center of most of Europe, with its policies on health care, welfare, worker rights, and the environment, is where American progressives would love to be.

Why Now?

Many reformers will quickly accept theoretical arguments for proportional representation, but question the viability of a PR movement. Some mistakenly think PR would require constitutional change or demand overly dramatic changes in our political culture. Others confuse PR with parliamentary government, although PR directly affects only how one elects a legislature, not governmental structure. Forms of PR could work extremely well with simple statutory changes, and a confluence of events in the 1990s provides a remarkable opportunity to work for PR's adoption. These developments include:

1. Winner-take-all politics that cannot be fixed. We have a particularly realistic opportunity to promote PR because of how well it addresses widely accepted failures in winner-take-all politics. Some of the most egregious problems reflect irreversible changes in technology, campaign techniques, and demographics. Without PR, no political reform—including the best of campaign finance reforms—can prevent most campaigns from being developed from focus groups of swing voters rather than principled policy positions. Campaign consultants know too much about how to win elections under winner-take-all rules. By freeing the majority to elect candidates they want, PR would weaken the stranglehold of the swing voters that give campaign consultants such power in winner-take-all elections.

2. Other reforms that face barriers. The most electorally successful political reform movement of the past decade has been the effort to put limits on the number of terms that legislators can serve. The Supreme Court has quashed term limits for congressional elections and may follow suit for state legislative elections. But the goals of term limit supporters are in any case only partly achieved by limits: most voters continue to live in one-party districts and to be frustrated by poll-driven politicians.

Moreover, for all the voter disgust with money in politics, campaign finance reformers now seem to be at an impasse at the federal level. The *Buckley v. Valeo* ruling, independent expenditures, and wealthy self-financed candidates bedevil reformers. Public financing supporters are making an expensive, potentially historic effort at the state level, and soon we will see how voters respond. But some analysts are skeptical that public financing can win in many states in the current climate of political depression. And even if it succeeds, the fundamental injustice of winner-take-all elections will remain. As Lani Guinier points out, it is not enough to take the money out of elections; we need PR to put the people in.

In any event, PR is an attractive complement to other reforms. And all of the reform energy that has developed in recent years provides an infrastructure of support for PR campaigns.

3. The opportunity to build a powerful coalition. As already discussed, women, racial minorities, advocates of

term limits and campaign finance reform, minor party supporters, and progressive constituencies within the Democratic Party all have particular incentives to support PR. Republicans also are facing growing splits, particularly on social issues, and losers in those internal Republican debates may be ready for opportunities to maintain and build representation with PR. The Center for Voting and Democracy is developing working relationships with representatives of most of these constituencies, who together form a majority coalition similar to those that developed in recent successful campaigns for PR in New Zealand and Scotland.

GETTING STARTED

Efforts to bring PR to American elections build on a rich history. Earlier this century two dozen cities, including Cincinnati, Cleveland, and New York, adopted the choice voting method of PR by initiative. Today's movement can learn much from this early PR movement. Choice voting was successful in achieving its reformers' primary goal: undercutting the power of one-party political machines. Unfortunately, this success led to these machines' unrelenting hostility. Although only two of the first 26 attempts to repeal choice voting in cities around the nation were successful, the previously dominant political forces eventually outlasted reformers and won repeals everywhere except Cambridge, Massachusetts. But the primary vehicles of anti-PR attacks—racist and anticommunist appeals and concerns about costly electoral administration—can be addressed far better today. PR activism is on the rise again. In 1995 and 1997, Representative Cynthia McKinney introduced a Voters' Choice Act to restore the option states had before 1967 to elect their congressional delegations by PR. The bill is gaining increasing attention from members, and other pro-PR legislation may soon be introduced in Congress. Several state groups have formed to promote PR, and recent PR initiatives in two major cities, Cincinnati and San Francisco, won 45 and 44 percent of the vote, respectively, despite limited funding and media exposure.

To be sure, many Americans—particularly elected officials—may be cautious about moving away from our political traditions. Moreover, much voter attention will continue to focus on "single-winner" executive offices—such as president, governor, and mayor—which do not allow for PR, since PR requires multiseat districts. Even so, there still are immediate opportunities to reform plurality methods that are used in most states.

Instant Runoffs

For executive offices, Australian-style instant runoff voting (IRV) would provide both better majority representation and minority participation than plurality voting. Australia uses IRV for parliamentary elections, Ireland uses it to elect its president, and the United Kingdom may well adopt it within two years in a national referendum on parliamentary elections. With IRV, voters rank candidates in order of choice: 1, 2, 3, and so on. Each voter still has only one vote, but ranking candidates allows the ballot count to simulate a series of runoff elections. If no candidate wins a majority of first-choice votes, the last-place candidate is eliminated. Ballots cast for that candidate are redistributed to each voter's next choice. This process of elimination occurs until a candidate wins majority support.

In the many states and localities still using traditional runoffs for primary or general elections, IRV would save money for taxpayers and campaign cash for candidates by combining two elections into one. Moreover, elected officials can appreciate IRV because it eliminates the "spoiler" problem created by minor parties—a problem for the major parties that the Reform Party and Green Party show great interest in expanding. And for minor parties, IRV reverses the "wasted vote" calculation. IRV allows minor party candidates to participate fully and potentially build their party's support. At the same time, Australia's experience with IRV demonstrates that it gives a minor party some leverage over major parties. A minor party candidate can call on supporters to hold back from casting second-choices for a major party candidate unless that candidate agrees to support some of the minor party's issues.

States that might well adopt IRV in the near future include Alaska, California, New Mexico, Pennsylvania, Texas, and Vermont. IRV could even be adopted for presidential elections by state legislation or initiative.

Three-Seat Districts

City, state, and national efforts for instant runoff voting would complement another modest modification of our rules that has the potential to draw support from the current political establishment: three-seat legislative districts with a 25 percent victory threshold.

From 1870 to 1980, Illinois used the semiproportional system of "cumulative voting" in three-seat districts to elect its lower house. Illinois elections were a modest departure from winner-take-all elections. Voters had three votes, but had the option to put all three votes on one candidate. If 25 percent of voters supported only one candidate, that candidate was sure to win. That is the mathematics of PR in a three-seat district: just over 25 percent wins one seat, just over 50 percent wins two, and over 75 percent of votes is necessary to sweep the district.

This relatively minor modification of winner-take-all rules had a profound impact on Illinois politics. Perhaps most significantly, nearly every constituency had two-party representation. Although most one-seat districts now are safe for one party, both in Illinois and around the nation, there are relatively few areas where at least 25 percent of voters are not ready to support another party—Bill Clinton won at least 25 percent of the vote in all U.S. House districts in 1996. A semiproportional system gives these minority voters a chance to win representation.

In Illinois, most constituencies typically had two representatives reflecting two major factions within the majority party and one representative from the smaller party. These minority-backed legislators played a creative role in the legislature. In 1995 the *Chicago Tribune* editorialized in support of cumulative voting's return, writing that "[M]any partisans and political independents have looked back wistfully at the era of cumulative voting. They acknowledge that it produced some of the best and brightest in Illinois politics."

The Center for Voting and Democracy recently commissioned a study of Illinois' use of a semiproportional system. Interviews with Illinois political leaders show strong bipartisan support for cumulative voting, including support from the state senate's majority leader and minority leader. A recurring theme is that semi-PR systems in three-seat districts actually provided better geographic representation than smaller, one-seat districts with monopoly representation. Constituents had more options when provided with access both to representatives in the majority party and the minority party. And both parties had direct interests in serving the needs of all parts of the state. The loss of cumulative voting has meant loss of bipartisan support for policies of particular interest to one-party strongholds; Chicago, for example, has been a big loser in equitable funding of public schools.

Three-seat districts are particularly promising as an alternative means to enforce the Voting Rights Act. If North Carolina adopted a proportional system with four three-seat districts for U.S. House elections, it would likely result in a greater number of competitive black candidates than the controversial redistricting plan that triggered several rulings against race-conscious districts around the nation. Such plans in the South also would increase representation of women and white moderates. Of 36 House members in the Deep South (South Carolina, Georgia, Alabama, Mississippi, and Louisiana), only one is a woman and only four are white Democrats.

Though cumulative voting has attractions, it also suffers from serious flaws, so we prefer either choice voting or an open party list system in such three-seat plans. Choice voting allows voters to rank candidates and have their votes coalesce behind candidates with the strongest support within major constituencies. In an open party list system, all votes for candidates from a particular party's "team" of candidates will boost the party's chances of winning seats.

As a first step toward change, we urge that states form commissions on reapportionment. These commissions could address issues such as: the number of legislators in a state; the problems deriving from the increased ability to gerrymander lines; and the potential of semi-PR and PR plans. An influential commission established in the mid-1980s in New Zealand surprised most political leaders by recommending replacement of the nation's winner-take-all system with a fully proportional system; that system was adopted by the voters in 1993 despite intense and well-financed opposition. Given the power of the argument for at least some modifications of winner-take-all elections, any commission with a degree of independence may well generate surprises in the United States as well.

Some Objections

To conclude, we consider some familiar objections to PR systems.

1. Political instability. True, Israel and Italy both use forms of PR and have faced problems of governmental instability. We could explore the historical and political complexities of these countries and their systems in order to exonerate the principle of PR, but suffice to say that most mature democracies with PR are not plagued by falling coalitions or right-wing religious parties. If we don't condemn winner-take-all elections by citing Alge-

ria, Pakistan, and India, then why condemn PR by citing Italy and Israel? There are currently 36 nations with more than two million people and high 1995 ratings from the human rights organization Freedom House. Of those 36, fully 30 use PR to elect their most powerful legislature, while only three—the United States, Canada, and Jamaica—elect all national bodies with a winner-take-all system.

2. Excessive gridlock. Some argue that we have enough gridlock with two parties and that adding more to the mix will simply make things worse. One answer to this concern again is empirical: nearly every major democracy has more than two-party representation, and most are not paralyzed by gridlock. In fact, many PR democracies—including Germany, Sweden, Netherlands, and Switzerland—have developed far more comprehensive policy than the United States on such major issues as health care and immigration. A two-party democracy rewards constant mudslinging and obstructionist posturing because if one party can drive up the negatives of the other, voters have only one place to go. "Zero sum politics" translates into "zero sum governance."

3. Loss of district representation. The advantage of district representation, it is said, is that all areas have someone to hold accountable for district issues. The problem is that most residents don't vote for their representatives and can't even identify them.

Furthermore, voters can take little comfort from being represented by someone who is sharply opposed to their own political philosophy. PR takes a different approach. All voters deserve an opportunity to choose a representative who thinks like them. With PR, voters find an ideological "home" rather than a geographic one. Their choice of representation may be influenced by local considerations, and systems can be designed to ensure some geographic representation, but geographic interests are not assumed to be paramount.

These three objections to PR do not exhaust the conventional list of concerns. But virtually every additional objection to PR, like those addressed here, is founded on the insulting theory that voters cannot handle the demands of making real choices. The typical winner-take-all advocate wants to keep things simple for the "poor bastards," who, left to their own devices, will keep electing unworkable governments and dangerous extremists. Empirical study and democratic principle condemn this charge. It is as objectionable as arguments against full suffrage.

We are skeptical, too, about arguments based on American exceptionalism. Yes, we are a continental democracy, with a unique constitution that makes accountability difficult, and long-standing traditions that should be modified with care. So we need to think hard about how best to realize the moral and political imperative of full representation. But that imperative itself retains its full and compelling force.

Committed democrats should act on it, and the ideal opportunity is quickly emerging. The redistricting process is the Achilles heel of our winner-take-all system. Behind closed doors, once every decade, the duopoly carves up the electorate, leaving most of us with another decade of no-choice legislative elections. The next gerrymandering is set for 2001. With 50 states as potential battlegrounds and voter frustration everywhere, a movement for PR has a perfect opening and a natural rallying cry that fits with its own democratic impulse: "This time let the voters decide."

2

KEEP IT SIMPLE

CYNTHIA MCKINNEY

In 1992, I experienced firsthand what it meant to largely rural African-Americans in Georgia for the first time in their lives to have a real hope of electing their candidate of choice to Congress. In 1996, my redesigned, now white-majority district returned many of my former constituents back to the old southern districts and left me, in the opinion of many analysts, little more than political roadkill. Contrary to the naysayers, I was able to win reelection in a tough campaign that demanded both great mobilization of African-American voters and sustained outreach to open-minded white constituents who had a chance to learn about me as an incumbent representative. "Fair representation of racial minorities" sounds good on paper, but believe me, it's far better in the real political world.

My experiences in mobilizing voters to win and then keep a seat in Congress helped me see that the reason for our low voter turnout and restless electorate go beyond a lack of reform in our campaign finance and lobbying systems. Voter choices on election day are usually so limited that when Americans find themselves going to the polls, all too often it is to vote against a candidate rather than for one. In a multimember district with proportional representation, voters would have a chance to choose among a range of viable candidates. A voter could likely support and elect a candidate who agreed with her on her issues of greatest concern—abortion rights, perhaps, or tax policy or child care—rather than having to settle for a lesser of two evils. I work hard to represent everyone in my district, but I have no illusions; a large number of my constituents would prefer another representative. And as the only congresswoman from Georgia and the only black woman representative from the Deep South states of South Carolina, Georgia, Alabama, Mississippi, and Louisiana, I feel an obligation to speak for many people outside my district. It is no different for my fellow Georgian Newt Gingrich and many other House members. PR would allow elections to be based on this reality, rather than the fallacy that members speak only for the people in their districts.

My experience in the 1990s certainly underlines the fact that districts are a construct of politics, not geography. The Rehnquist Supreme Court has argued that the politics of districting allow districts to be gerrymandered "bizarrely" to protect white incumbents, but not to promote representation of black and minority voters. Rob Richie and Steven Hill are right on target when they suggest that redistricting allows legislators to choose their constituents before their constituents choose them.

Critics of race-conscious districting who suggest that race is the only cause of gerrymandering—and only a problem if blacks become a majority in a district—are either astoundingly naive or dangerously manipulative. Whatever tools were used in 1991 to 1992 to draw black-majority districts were applied with far greater vigor to create "safe" districts to protect white incumbents from their constituents.

Most of the democratic world long ago abandoned one-seat district representation. In 1996, South Africa cemented its rejection of one-seat districts when President Nelson Mandela signed a new constitution with a requirement for proportional representation. It is impressive that 33 of the world's 36 major, full-fledged democracies use forms of PR.

I have long been convinced of the merits of PR, which is why I introduced the Voters' Choice Act in Congress in 1995 and again in 1997. The Voters' Choice Act (HR 3068) is a modest but very important step toward promoting serious debate about PR in the United States. It would restore the opportunity for states to use PR systems to elect their delegations to the U.S. House of Representatives. Its potential appeal is broad enough that in announcing my 1995 bill, I had beside me the directors of U.S. Term Limits, the Committee for the Study of the American Electorate, and the National Women's Political Caucus.

The political establishment in Washington has a difficult time with PR because it requires that its members earn their power, not inherit it. The Voters' Choice Act faces an uphill battle. The political imperative of history demands that we take action, however. Women's suffrage began as a so-called unrealistic idea, as did the concept of democracy itself. Yet today these precepts are so firmly rooted in our polity that they seem almost part of our societal DNA. The discussion on PR must begin in earnest as public discontent increases, voter turnout decreases, and political minorities come under siege in our halls of power. It is high time to challenge the "winner-take-all" notion that a candidate securing 50.1 percent of the votes deserves 100 percent of power.

While I am thus convinced by the authors' arguments for PR in the United States, as a political practitioner I have three suggestions:

1. Describe PR more simply. I agree with Richie and Hill that PR has much appeal to supporters of term limits, voting rights, and campaign finance reform. But not only these Americans must understand PR; advocates must learn to explain it in a way that a second-grader can understand it. One of my favorite examples is shopping for cereal. As consumers Americans enjoy a wide variety of choice in cereal. We would be outraged if we had to choose only between corn flakes or shredded wheat. Yet our electorate is settling for even less variety: on election day Americans essentially get a choice between corn flakes or frosted flakes. They are the same thing; one is

just a little sweeter than the other. PR would put more variety, and spice, in our electoral diet.

2. Show incumbents the merits in PR. For PR to become a reality for elections in most state legislatures and Congress, incumbent legislators need to see its value for them. I am encouraged by support for the principle of minority representation found in Illinois. In addition to learning more about the history of cumulative voting in Illinois and the past and current history of PR in other American elections, PR advocates must explain what positive changes PR would make for incumbents. One important change relates to redistricting. Many members of Congress are already preparing for the next redistricting after the 2000 census, knowing that their political lives may be at stake. Conversion to PR would allow them to earn a loyal constituency and the power to control their own destiny, since by serving their constituencies well they can earn reelection

3. Make voting rights central. I was very pleased that the National Black Caucus of State Legislators recently adopted a resolution to study PR. The historic struggle for the voting rights of blacks, Latinos, Asian-Americans, and Native Americans provides a legacy upon which PR advocates must build. Our message must be simple: we cannot go back. If the Supreme Court limits majority-minority districts, then we will find another way. PR may be just the alternative approach that our times demand.

CAUTIONARY NOTES

JOHN FEREJOHN

Richie and Hill argue that democratic justice requires proportional representation. Single-member district systems of election are, in their view, fundamentally defective: they are insufficiently representative, and they artificially reduce the options for voter choice, thus limiting the range of viewpoints present in the legislature and emasculating political debate and discussion. This reduction in the range of viable candidates diminishes the representation of minorities and historically underrepresented groups (such as women) and tends to reduce voter turnout as well. In addition, single-member district (SMD) systems permit and encourage officials to gerrymander electoral districts in order to increase their own job security at the expense of making most legislative contests uncompetitive. Richie and Hill argue, moreover, that such systems cannot be reformed by regulating campaign finance, limiting incumbent control over redistricting, or redrawing districts with a view to fixing problems of "misrepresentation," both because such reforms are politically unfeasible and because they do not touch the root defects of SMD systems. The authors argue that there are proportional representation systems that would cure these defects, and that there is a politically practical path that can bring about a transition to such a system. Richie and Hill thus present three arguments: that SMD systems are incurably defective, that there are superior PR systems, and that the adoption of PR is politically practical.

I think it is possible to agree with many of the criticisms of SMD systems. There is no question that SMD systems limit the range of representatives that can be elected. It seems clear that racial and ethnic minorities and women are probably not elected in the numbers they would be under other electoral systems, and this fact of underrepresentation probably does contribute to limiting the kind of debate that takes place in American legislatures. It is important to emphasize, however, that other ideological or religious minorities are probably underrepresented as well and these voices would probably appear in greater abundance in PR elected legislatures. In this respect, one of the conditions for full legislative deliberation—a wide range of viewpoints—would be enhanced. What viewpoints would be expressed would depend, of course, on which interests organized themselves into parties for purposes of presenting candidates for election. It is also not clear that meaningful legislative deliberation would actually increase, however, since many of these new voices would likely be tied very closely to narrow ideological constituencies and may not be as willing or able to engage in political accommodation as are current legislators.

I think the authors' suggestion that SMD systems depress turnout relative to PR systems is somewhat less convincing. Even if one grants that PR offers voters more of a chance to elect candidates they prefer, the magnitude of this effect on turnout appears to be very small. Moreover, it is not at all clear that the individual voter's influence on the ultimate policy produced by the legislature is larger in one system than another. The cross-national comparisons offered by Richie and Hill seem unconvincing when we consider the many other confounding factors—that some nations penalize nonvoting, for example, or that the United States, with more than half a million officials, has many more elections than virtually any other modern nation—as well as the cultural differences between countries. Further, many SMD systems have very high turnout rates: the United Kingdom and France average about 75 percent, and New Zealand voters turned out at almost a 90 percent rate when that country employed SMD elections. Poland employs PR, has a wide range of parties in the legislature (including one called the Beer Drinkers Party), and has a lower turnout rate than the United States.

I also agree with the authors that many of the defects of SMD systems are intransigient and not very susceptible to reform. They are traceable more to the way the population is distributed geographically, rather than to the real but marginal effects of the incumbency advantage, campaign spending distortions, or gerrymandering. It is just hard to see many Republicans getting elected from central cities or Democrats from the non–urban South, almost no matter how the districts are drawn. Thus, even if campaign finance were to be reformed, gerrymandering eliminated, and term limits imposed, it would still be the case that SMD systems would tend to produce at most two viable candidates in most districts, and a high proportion of relatively uncompetititive seats. Given the geographic distribution of minorities, minority underrepresentation in legislatures would no doubt persist (although this is probably more attributable to historical biases in intraparty nomination processes than to the use of SMD elections), though it is less clear that underrepresentation of women would. Thus, if one is concerned, as the authors are, with enhancing "descriptive representation" (making the legislature look like the electorate) or fuller legislative deliberation (making the legislature sound like the electorate), reforming the electoral system the direction of PR seems an attractive way to go.

I also agree with the authors that the political impediments to such a change are probably less formidable than they might appear. Single-member districting is not constitutionally entrenched, and within many states could be implemented through use of the popular initiative. Implementation at the congressional level would require only statutory change. And, while the authors might be right that a broad progressive coalition might be fabricated for these purposes, I think it as likely that many on the religious right and economic libertarians might find the idea just as attractive. I have rather less hope that a congressional majority, elected under the current system, would be swayed by such a movement— it will hardly appear to be the most pressing political issue even for the members of a reform coalition, since their attraction to PR will be largely instrumental—and I have similar doubts about the prospects for such reform in states without the popular initiative. But, in many parts of the country, PR-oriented reform might well be politically viable and perhaps worth experimenting with.

I am not yet convinced, however, that Richie and Hill have made a case for adopting PR all things considered, because they have not addressed the new problems that PR would likely produce. It is possible, of course, that it is worth adopting PR despite its weaknesses, but that argument needs to be made explicitly. The authors are remarkably casual in dismissing what I take to be the main problems with PR systems, saying that concerns about accountability, transparency, and governability are "insulting" to voters and "as objectionable as arguments against full suffrage." They also cursorily dismiss the experiences of Italy and Israel with PR systems suggesting without argument that these experiences are atypical. This failure to give arguments about the attractiveness of

PR all things considered is unhelpful for two reasons. First, it is not clear that Israel and Italy are that atypical. One could list as well the French Fourth Republic and Weimar Germany as other instances in which PR systems may have produced circumstances of chronic constitutional conflict. Second, and more importantly, the refusal to analyze actual PR experiences limits our capacity to understand why some PR systems failed and how reformers in this country might avoid those fates. The framers of the German Basic Law and of the Constitution of the French Fifth Republic certainly had theories about what was wrong with the Weimar and Fourth Republic electoral systems, and they attempted to remedy these defects by adopting electoral systems that were less than fully proportional (the French adopted SMDs, while the Germans chose a mixed system with relatively high representational thresholds).

To me, the principal defect of PR is the weakness of electoral responsiveness—the relationship between electoral expressions of public opinion and public policy. PR systems tend to produce fragmented electoral outcomes in which no party wins a majority of seats and, for that reason, interparty coalitions are required to enact legislation (or to form governments in parliamentary systems). Electoral shifts in popular support for or against a party, in such circumstances, typically do not much alter the logic of coalition formation so that similar or identical coalitions may reform even after substantial electoral shifts. The continuous presence of the Christian Democrats in postwar Italian governments is only the most notorious example of this rather ubiquitous phenomenon. As a result, electoral results are often not reflected in policy outcomes (or government composition). In this sense, PR governments are "too stable."

In another sense, however, the logic of coalition formation in multiparty systems is inherently unstable in the sense that governing coalitions can shift independently of electorally expressed preferences. The frequent breakdowns of governing coalitions in Fourth Republic France and postwar Italy (or Weimar, or Israel, or Poland) are again not atypical. Insofar as PR produces multiparty outcomes (and, as the modern German case indicates, this tendency can be limited by adopting representational thresholds or other institutional checks on PR), the problem of limited electoral responsiveness is real and can produce problems of legitimacy. I must say that I don't see how it is insulting to voters to mention this. Such tendencies are simply operating characteristics of certain kinds of PR systems. Is it insulting to voters to point out the incentives of politicians to gerrymander in SMD systems? The voter's could, if they chose, punish incumbents for such behavior.

Finally I want to return to the issue of the amount and kind of deliberation fostered by the two electoral arrangements. It is well to remember that, in the end, the legislature will only adopt one policy and that all those who dislike this policy will be disappointed at the stage of policy choice. PR systems, by increasing descriptive representation, bring more diverse voices into the legislature and require that political arguments about policies happen in the public legislative forum. However, by encouraging wide ranging debate to occur within a broadly representative legislature, PR encourages a politics of mobilization rather than persuasion within the electorate. This, indeed, is why Richie and Hill claim that PR will increase turnout. SMD systems, by contrast, force compromise and accomodation to occur within the electoral process, putting weight on persuading what the authors call "swing voters" (others use the term "median voters") within the district, and produce a less diverse but possibly more tractable legislature. In effect, the legislative diversity in SMD legislatures is due to interdistrict differences whereas that in PR legislatures arises both from intradistrict and interdistrict variation. Policy choice is presumably easier (and more transparent) in SMD systems because many of the underlying social conflicts have already been implicitly accomodated earlier in the process.

There is little question that SMD systems have some real defects, especially with regard to the representation of minorities. But PR systems have weaknesses too and it is no accident that many countries have moved away from the purer forms of PR in reaction to particular unhappy experiences. I think that because PR systems promise to remedy some of the defects of SMD systems, it is particularly important that we experiment with the most attractive versions, ones that do not cause other, possibly worse, problems. Doing this requires paying careful attention to the experiences of other jurisdictions with such systems—yes, even Italy and Israel—in order to take advantage of the most attractive features of PR systems while avoiding their weaknesses.

SOLVING A LEGAL PUZZLE

E. JOSHUA ROSENKRANZ

Clarence Thomas and Lani Guinier don't agree on much. So when the archconservative Supreme Court justice and the Clinton nominee who was dumped as too radical find common ground, we should take notice. Both agree that some version of proportional representation is an attractive way out of one of the most mind-numbing legal and philosophical puzzles of democratic representation.

Suppose a state with a racially polarized electorate wants to increase the representation of racial minorities in its legislature or congressional contingent. The state might want to do that because the Voting Rights Act, as amended in 1982, requires the government to arrange elections in a way that gives racial minorities a realistic opportunity to elect a representative of their choice. Or it might want to do that because it believes that, as a matter of fairness, a white majority ought to share its power with racial minorities. What should it do?

The traditional solution has been to draw race-conscious single-member districts. That means the government divides the voters into discrete districts, each of which elects one representative. The white majority continues to dominate most of the districts, but the lines are drawn so as to cordon off one or two districts in which the racial minority predominates. The result is often an oddly shaped district whose voters share little in common except for their race.

North Carolina is a good illustration. Almost a quarter of the state's population is nonwhite. But its voters are so racially polarized that any district with a white majority would not elect an African-American. So long as districts were drawn to submerge the black minority, the state sent only white representatives to Congress. To avoid a Justice Department prosecution under the Voting Rights Act, the state redrew a couple of districts, linking together predominantly black neighborhoods; sure enough, those districts elected African-American representatives. The districts weren't pretty though. One of them snaked for 160 miles along a highway from Charlotte to Durham. The joke was that you could drive down Interstate 85 with both doors open and hit most of the people in the district.

Pretty or not, the technique, applied across the nation, profoundly altered the complexion of state legislatures and Congress. The number of African-Americans elected to office nationwide increased by almost 20 percent and the number of Latinos increased by 50 percent between 1985 and 1992. In 1992, of the 16 new black members who were elected to Congress, 13 came from districts that had been redrawn to encompass black majorities.

However laudable these results, the means of achieving them are intensely controversial. Critics decry race-conscious districting as bowing to the fallacies that skin color dictates political interest and that only an African-American representative could represent a black constituency well. "Racial balkanization," as Justice Thomas has called it, discourages people of different races from trying to find common ground. Even those who have favored enhancing the power of racial minorities worry that packing all the blacks in one district reduces their influence in the surrounding districts. And the practice has occasionally sparked feuds between different racial or ethnic minorities who would draw different lines to maximize their own power.

An increasingly conservative Supreme Court is among the detractors, casting doubt on the future of race-conscious districting. White voters have brought a spate of lawsuits in the wake of redistricting in the early 1990s, alleging that the drawing of race-conscious lines violated their right to equal protection. Accepting this claim, the Court struck North Carolina's meandering district because, in Justice Sandra Day O'Connor's ill-chosen words, it smacked of "political apartheid." "Racial gerrymandering, even for remedial purposes," she wrote for the Court, "may balkanize us into competing racial factions . . . [and] carry us further from the goal of a political system in which race no longer matters."

That does not mean that legislators who draw districts cannot think about race. To the contrary, the Voting Rights Act still commands them to concern themselves with race when they draw their districts. The Court has just declared that race cannot be the "predominant factor" in drawing a district—whatever that means. "Think about race, but not too much," is the governing principle. So long as single-member districts are the rule, legislatures will be at their peril in drawing lines. And every effort to walk the tightrope is a potential Supreme Court case.

The voting rights quandary mirrors the battle about racial preferences that has bitterly divided the country in other contexts. The public favors opportunities for the disadvantaged and does not mind race-neutral approaches that happen to benefit racial minorities disproportionately, but both the public and the courts are increasingly hostile to preferences linked expressly to race.

If Justice Thomas had his way, race would be an entirely impermissible factor, whether in employment or in drawing districts. But in a recent case, he offered a solution to the puzzle in the voting rights context. "In principle," he said, "cumulative voting and other non-district-based methods of effecting proportional representation are simply more efficient and straightforward mechanisms for achieving what has already become our tacit objective: roughly proportional allocation of political power according to race." That's right: Justice Thomas, perhaps facetiously, is promoting Lani Guinier's proposal to turn toward cumulative voting and other techniques for increasing the voting power of racial minorities.

The two have put their fingers on one of the great benefits of PR of any flavor, whether cumulative voting, limited voting, or preference voting. It empowers racial or ethnic minorities—indeed, minorities of any sort—without taking stock of race or ethnicity. With PR, it almost doesn't matter how you draw the lines, or whether you do away with lines altogether and run all candidates at large. As Rob Richie and Steven Hill cogently demonstrate, under PR, minority preferences will emerge in rough proportion to their numbers and intensity. Predictably, jurisdictions nationwide that have adopted PR have shown dramatic increases in election rates of minority-preferred candidates, because these alternative approaches drive down the threshold of exclusion—the proportion of votes a particular candidate must attract in order to win a seat.

What's more, PR does not depend upon any of the philosophically divisive assumptions that undermine support for race-based districting. The state does not group voters by race on the assumption that skin color dictates political interests. Rather, the voters essentially group themselves, in what Guinier calls "districts of the mind." And since they do, there is no reason to fear that political strength in one area is bought at the price of weakness in the surrounding areas or that one racial minority can be empowered only to the detriment of another.

These benefits were enough to persuade numerous locales to adopt PR as a way of settling nettlesome voting rights complaints rather than the usual remedy of redrawing the map. A handful of federal judges have even gone so far as to order jurisdictions to adopt cumulative voting to remedy voting rights violations. Whether or not federal courts have such broad remedial powers, the unease caused by current law on race-conscious districting should be enough to convince state and local legislatures to experiment with models of PR in their elections and to convince Congress to free states to do the same for congressional races. There may be pitfalls, but if both Guinier and Thomas buy it, perhaps it's worth a try.

INSTABILITY?

GARY W. COX

The United States has a presidential system of government. This simple—and constitutionally entrenched—fact has profound implications for any project to reform our electoral system. It is one thing to push a parliamentary system, such as New Zealand or the United Kingdom, toward proportional representation. It is quite another to push a presidential system in the same direction. I would argue that any such push should be limited—as is, for example, Richie and Hill's current proposal of three-seat districts operating under the single transferable vote system.

The argument for limiting the move to PR goes as follows: first, PR tends to promote multipartyism; second, multiparty presidential regimes have in practice performed poorly. As the first point—that PR facilitates multipartyism—is not in dispute, I shall focus on the second.

That multiparty presidential regimes have in fact performed poorly is evident from the Latin American record. Chile (1932–1973) is the only case of a multiparty presidential system lasting more than a quarter century.

All the other examples of long-lived presidential democracy—Colombia, Costa Rica, pre-1973 Uruguay, and Venezuela—come from systems with long spells of two-partyism.

The reason generally offered to explain why multiparty presidentialism works poorly is that such systems typically deprive the president of a working majority in the legislature, resulting in ineffective and gridlock-prone "divided government." In Latin America, this has even contributed to attempts to govern by presidential decree (for example, Collor in Brazil) and coups d'état (for example, Fujimori in Peru).

In the United States, divided government has not had such dramatic consequences but some of the same tendencies can be seen. I shall consider just two examples: budget deficits and "unilateralism."

The enormous budget deficit of the early 1980s—one of the defining issues of U.S. politics in the past twenty years—has been blamed in part on the fact that government was divided under Ronald Reagan's presidency. A simple thought experiment suggests the line of argument: first, had Reagan had a firm majority of Republicans in Congress in place for the 1982 budget, the deficit might still have increased (due to the big increase in defense spending combined with tax cuts) but it would not have ballooned by as much as it did (because he would have made substantial cuts in social spending); second, had Jimmy Carter managed to defeat Reagan in 1980, again there might have been a deficit but it would not have been as large: the Democrats would not have increased defense spending by as much nor would they have cut taxes. Under divided government, however, the two parties' opposing interests led to a triple threat to fiscal prudence—greatly increased defense spending, large tax cuts, no cuts in social spending—and hence the largest deficits as a percent of GDP in our history outside of wartime. This tendency of divided governments to produce larger budget deficits has been confirmed in studies of the U.S. states and of bicameral institutions in Europe.

Another tendency that can be observed under divided government in the United States is for both parties to pursue their policy objectives unilaterally, to the extent that they are able. For the party controlling the presidency, this has meant attempts to expand the institutional powers of the presidency (e.g., Nixon's attempt to expand the power of impoundment in the early 1970s) or to use executive orders rather than statutes to implement policies (e.g., Bush's "gag rule" forbidding federally funded family planning counselors to mention the option of abortion). Perhaps the most extended example of unilateralism at both ends of Pennsylvania Avenue occurred during the 100th Congress, when President Reagan and Speaker of the House Jim Wright conducted what amounted to separate and incompatible foreign policies toward the Sandinista regime in Nicaragua—

each side using powers and strategies that did not require the consent of the other.

The general point is this: a highly proportional electoral system to elect the legislature, when combined with presidentialism, will enhance the chances of getting divided government. While power-sharing governments of some forms are extolled as desirable—particularly in the literature on "consociationalism"[1]—divided presidential regimes have some undesirable features. The key problem from my perspective has to do with what happens when power-sharing politicians cannot agree on a compromise. Under a parliamentary regime, when coalition partners cannot agree on a sufficiently important matter, the government falls: the top political leaders lose their positions, or at least put them at immediate risk, and appeal to public opinion to resolve the impasse. Thus, part of the pain for failing to arrive at an acceptable compromise falls immediately on politicians. Contrast this to what happens in the United States when we fail to pass a budget before the close of the fiscal year. No politician immediately loses office. The electoral consequences may turn out to be substantial—arguably the budget impasse of 1995 hurt Bob Dole's 1996 presidential bid—but they are not immediate. The only immediate pain that arose as a consequence of failure to agree on a budget compromise fell on various civil servants and users of government services. Not only can presidents and assemblies defy one another without fear of immediate loss of position in presidential regimes, but they both can claim a direct mandate from the people. The bargaining incentives in presidential regimes more often lead to delay and brinkmanship, public shouting matches, and the burning of bridges. Public dispute between elites is a precious thing, not to be done away with by any means. But there is such a thing as too much of a good thing.

Given that converting our system from a presidential to a parliamentary one is not at all likely at present, electoral reformers need to accept presidentialism as a given and react accordingly. Especially those who dislike the status quo (whether progressives or reactionaries) will want to make sure that a single reasonably cohesive majority coalition could in principle emerge under a proposed new electoral system. Otherwise, bold new departures in any direction are rendered unlikely.

MAKING IT HAPPEN

DANIEL CANTOR

When the New Party brought the "fusion" case *McKenna v. Twin Cities New Party* to the Supreme Court in April 1996, we did so because we felt that fusion (the ability of more than one party to nominate the same candidate on separate ballot lines) was the historic American answer to the question that in other countries is answered by proportional representation: how can minority political opinion be represented in governance? Granted, PR is a more powerful reform than fusion, but fusion (unlike PR) could be established nationwide by the votes of five reasonably fair-minded Supreme Court justices. Unfortunately, as we discovered when the Court announced its decision, there are currently only three. As a result of that ruling, the fusion option is gone, at least in most states, at least for now. The need for pro-minor party electoral reform remains, however, and PR has got to be in the toolbox of any serious democratic activist, intellectual, or donor.

That PR is coming alive, albeit slowly, is entirely a testament to the will and skill of Rob Richie, Steve Hill, and their allies in the Center for Voting and Democracy.

No one would even be talking about PR if it weren't for them. They are true democrats.

They also have written a marvelous piece. I thought I knew the basic reasons to favor PR—it's fairer; it's good for minority voters (whether they be minorities in terms of race, politics, or just plain arithmetic); and it improves the caliber of debate (not hard to do in America, but that's another story). But I don't think I fully appreciated just how powerful PR would be and how useful it would be for the left were it to be reestablished.

Richie and Hill hit the mark on so-called "swing voters . . . the relatively few voters with so little political grounding that they will support either party." Often considered savvy for their unwillingness to be pigeonholed as supporters of one party or another, and always the sought-after targets of the pernicious campaign consultants, swing voters are absurdly influential in our winner-take-all system, which demands that candidates tailor campaigns to their wobbly minds. Over time, PR would reduce their silly stranglehold on our elections, as it would increase turnout, reduce the wasted vote problem, and permit ideas from "the wings" to be heard. Indeed, if I read Richie and Hill right, government policies under a PR system will still trend toward the "center," but that center itself is likely to shift to the left once the views of the sociological majority (most notably, labor and its allies) are able to be heard by the citizenry and reflected in state economic policy.

The response to this argument from some factions of the Democratic Party will be that U.S. politics would more likely shift even farther right under PR (for example, Pat Robertson doing to President Kemp what the religious parties in Israel do to the Likud). PR in this view is dangerous experimentation. Richie and Hill have more confidence in ordinary people, and I'm with them. Everyone gets to play in democracy, it's true, but there is a huge market for a sensible, progressive, let's-not-have-corporations-rule-the-entire-world politics, and PR helps us reach the market.

Making it happen will take a huge effort. Organizations will still have to do the work, and key allies will have to be found inside the progressive wing of the Democratic Party, because they would greatly benefit from PR (even if they don't understand that yet). A genuine "threat of exit" would help progressive Democrats in intraparty bargaining. (The Center for Voting and Democracy has already started to make some of these connections, particularly with the Congressional Black Caucus.)

But the real play is at the municipal level, and it's not yet clear how PR can win over existing officeholders who would live in a more interesting—possibly more progressive, but also more unstable—political environment. Elected officials in most municipalities will be less than enthusiastic about a system that decreases the relative power of candidates vis-à-vis their party or slate, and this problem will hold across all racial groups. That would seem to leave only the tried and true avenue of a charter amendment or ballot initiative, which Richie and Hill tell us is on the agenda for consideration in at least a few cities right now. The task will be how to persuade the grantmakers funding state-level campaign finance reform to back PR as well; Richie and Hill's article makes a strong case that it is at least as important as campaign finance, and perhaps even more so.

Of course, convincing the funders is only one problem that PR advocates face, which brings me back to the fusion case. During the oral argument, Justice Breyer asked why the Supreme Court should require states to allow fusion—since, after all, the Court doesn't require proportional representation, and everyone knows that winner-take-all elections are an even greater obstacle to minor parties. Proving once again that our enemies fully understand why changes in the rules of the game are the ones they absolutely have to block. We might as well force them to do so, because the outcome might surprise us all.

MIXING THE MESSAGE

ROSS MIRKARIMI

Rob Richie and Steve Hill make a good case for the virtues of proportional representation as a cure for the ills
of an American electoral system driven by the evil of two
lessers (Democrats/Republicans). But they stop short of
identifying and addressing the problems associated with
the politics of electoral reform.

The fundamental difficulty for a PR movement today in the United States is not its ideological content but
the form in which its message is delivered. To succeed,
the movement must build a bridge from the language of
democratic theory to the pragmatic language of political
change. Though Americans often view change as necessary, it also makes us nervous. So a campaign designed
to shift from a "winner-take-all" system to an improved,
"state-of-the-art" brand of democracy will require the
work of skilled communicators—those who can present
their message concisely and give the appearance that
they are David fighting Goliath. Organizers of the dar-
ing 1996 San Francisco ballot initiative campaign
("Proposition H"), which sought to institute a PR-type
system of preferential voting, managed to win support

from all sectors of the populace prior to receiving the perfunctory blessing of our one-party, one-machine town. That was a major achievement, with important lessons for other campaigns. But while "H" came close, it did not win—partly because of the difficulty proponents had in distilling its message. (The lack of resources didn't help.)

A key ingredient in the message of the PR movement should be increased voter turnout. As the struggle for democracy in Europe and throughout the rest of the world has reached its most inspiring level since 1848, large numbers of citizens in the world's oldest democracy do not vote. In 1988, only 50.1 percent of eligible voters went to the polls. In 1992, Ross Perot's careening appeal to people who felt themselves cut off from politics as usual helped bring 104 million citizens (55 percent of the voting-age population) to the polls. This figure was encouraging, but it hardly represented a sudden return to civic engagement after three decades of voter indifference.

Perot fizzled. Clinton and the "new" Democrats have been busy trying to look like the Republicans, while the Republicans are not sure what they look like. Meanwhile, on the third-party front, the Greens and the New Party struggle to stay out of the 3 percent club, while the Christian Right unleashes its stealth technology of grassroots conviction. These new political groups want to expand the pool of voters. By allying themselves with

these forces in a campaign to revitalize citizen participation, PR advocates could find a home in partisan politics, especially third-party efforts that range from left to
right. By putting partisan energies behind reform efforts
designed to increase turnout, reformers increase the
chances of political success.

But voter turnout is not just about numbers. Turnout
has dropped in part because of the disappearance of the
old party-machine and ward system, whose last vestige
was Mayor Daley's Chicago. Whatever their abuses, machines got people—street by street, household by household—to the voting booth, and the patronage system
helped tie Americans, especially blue-collar and lower-
middle-class people, to the belief that citizens have a role
to play in running their municipalities and their country—from the bottom up, district by district. It rein-
forced the sense of participatory democracy. PR advocates know that the less the poor vote, the more the party
of the rich will benefit. So increasing voter turnout will
help to overcome the rule of the rich. If PR campaigns
learn how to connect their message of electoral reform to
the message of economic exclusion, they stand a fair
chance of winning.

For political theorists, the more reasons for PR the
better. For political campaigns, a simple but compelling
message will suffice.

COME OUT FIGHTING

Richie and Hill make a compelling case for the importance of PR as a major component of electoral reform in the United States. I accept their basic argument that "winner-take-all" election rules limit party competition, suppress voter participation, narrow the scope of public debate, and minimize the representation of women and racial and ideological minorities, thus undermining "representative" government and marginalizing progressive electoral politics. On basic measures of participation, accountability, and free and open debate, our current electoral system is a sham. And by any measure, a stable progressive electoral politics does not exist in the United States. Both of these tacts can be explained in large part by the absence of PR.

Conversely, a PR universe would be a healthier and more exciting one. Especially in the urban context with which I am most familiar, PR would enable much more successful navigation of the shifting racial and ethnic composition of our metropolitan areas. It would promote greater accountability from elected officials including those "progressive" ones we occasionally elect, only to watch them often drift off in a blur of campaign contributions and personally directed machine building, tailoring their reelection efforts to the small universe of "likely" voters. And, by permitting effective expression of minority ideological views, it would give footing to reconstructive efforts more plausible than "business as usual." My own efforts with the fledgling Metropolitan Alliance in Los Angeles, for example, persuade me that a representative and open politics would find majority support among residents for tax and economic development policies diametrically opposed to those now imposed by the powers-that-be. That majority is unlikely ever to find its voice, however, in our current system of political districting. If we change that system in the way that PR could, a whole new political world would indeed come into view.

But as Richie and Hill also note, none of these arguments or observations is new. The more immediate argument that is needed, then, is a political one—why reforms clearly beneficial to developing an authentic democracy have not been made, and why we think they might be made now.

Richie and Hill offer very little analysis on the first part of this puzzle, but they speculate on the second. As I understand them, some combination of adverse Supreme Court decisions on race-based districting, general citizen alienation from politics, and the frustrations now encountered by other electoral reform movements (particularly those for term limits and campaign finance) makes the moment right for a PR reform movement. PR offers a workable solution to our contested race politics, an inducement to political action for currently disaffected voters, and a reform more fundamental and appealing than those currently resisted or under attack.

None of this makes much sense to me, however, unless more is said about the sort of coalition that might emerge around PR, the role of ideology in shaping "majority" consciousness, and the forces that are likely to resist its efforts.

Beginning with the last, Richie and Hill are virtually silent on those who have good reasons to resist PR. They observe that "[a]nyone who supports fuller democracy and is willing to accept the verdict of a fully realized majority should be supportive of PR elections." But they say next to nothing about the extent and power of those who oppose exactly that "fuller democracy." Who are these antidemocrats, who benefit from the current de-democratization of the United States and can reasonably be expected not only to tolerate, but to fight to preserve, a less than fully realized democracy?

Their ranks of course include most incumbent members of both political parties (including, sadly, many minority elected officials). The power of two-party incumbents would clearly be diminished by a representative system, and in the 26 states that do not permit citizen initiatives or binding referenda, they have a monopoly on legislative power.

Important as they are, however, elected officials are only small fry. The more formidable opponent is the business "community" that currently controls them and the rest of our politics. Corporate interests effectively own both major parties, along with the media that interprets the world for us. They certainly have the resources, especially in our system of campaign finance, to make or break almost any individual candidate. And they are doing just fine, thank you, without a "fully realized" democracy. I know of no Los Angeles businessperson who wants everyone in LA to vote, much less vote with good information about a wide range of political alternatives. For them, even our currently feeble democracy is an annoyance; a fully realized one would be a threat of the first order.

Richie and Hill may accept all this, but they don't seem to draw the natural conclusion: that advancing PR will be a colossal fight, pitting the powers-that-aren't against the powers-that-be. Nor do they consider the natural question that follows from that conclusion: How can we mobilize and keep intact our core base for this effort? I think the core pro-PR coalition that needs to be assembled is not most usefully described as "nonpartisan," but as working class, minority, female, and poor.

And I think its real end should not be described as PR per se, but instead a more fully realized democracy itself, centrally including some real political power exercised on its own behalf. And I think that that coalition's success requires some unifying program (beyond PR itself) on the ends to which its power might be exercised, as well as the support of those organizations (unions, community groups, and so on) that are currently organizing and representing its members.

Of course, such a project will inevitably be messier and more oppositional than what Richie and Hill seem to have in mind. But for those with a stake in PR, I don't see any alternative. I'm not against quoting John Stuart Mill, or reminding ruling elites that their legitimacy should depend on broad voter validation of their policies, of the sort the present system does not deliver. But since I don't think most elites care about such democratic validation, I doubt the effectiveness of such argument. Conversely, the fact that those with the most to gain from PR have other grounds for unity is a good thing, a source of cohesion in what in the best of circumstances will be a protracted struggle for electoral reform. Not recognizing and accommodating that would amount to confusing intellectual agreement on the requirements of "representative government" with their practical satisfaction.

In the end, authentic or full democracy is not an abstract or nonpartisan concept. It is grounded in questions of democracy for whom and with what rights. The history of the development of democracy as a political system has been the history of struggle between elite forces in society and various oppressed/exploited social constituencies (workers, minorities, women). Moving PR as an issue I think requires integrating it into a broader democratic project, framed by the needs of those who are asked to carry it forward and would most benefit from its implementation.

A BIGGER PICTURE

PAMELA S. KARLAN

There's a paradox at the core of democratic politics. We use elections to tally up our preferences and to determine the future direction and structure of our government, but existing arrangements powerfully influence our preferences and dramatically limit the choices available to us. The kind of democracy we have, and can imagine, is thus quite path-dependent, like the famous Escher print of a hand drawing itself drawing a hand.

I want to draw out two key points implicit in Rob Richie and Steven Hill's illuminating discussion of proportional representation. The first is that it's impossible to talk about any of the critical problems that beset the American electoral system without ultimately having to talk about all of them. Low voter turnout, an incumbent retention rate that rivals the Soviet Union's at its height, campaign finance scandals, the turmoil over the role of race in the redistricting process, a legislative inability or unwillingness to confront and solve difficult questions of public policy, and so on: they're all connected, at least in part.

For example, if elections were more competitive, there might not be so much pressure for term limits, which threaten to replace incumbents not with the vaunted citizen-legislators of the eighteenth century but with a herd of amateurs uninterested in considering the long term because they won't be around to be held accountable. If officials were not squeezed by the need for constant fundraising, they might spend more time responding to the viewpoints of the mainstream of their constituencies. If large numbers of liberal and moderate whites didn't view the attempt to give minority voters a fair chance to elect the candidates they prefer as a nefarious right-wing plot to benefit the Republican Party, they might ask how to rebuild a New Deal–style coalition, but this time with blacks as full participants.

The second key point is how very contingent the American form of democracy is. Most Americans are woefully ignorant about alternative democratic arrangements, particularly those that involve some form of proportional representation. The movement toward democracy has swept around the world in the past few decades. While the movement has been inspired in large part by American ideals, only a small handful of emerging democracies in Eastern and Central Europe, Asia, or South Africa has adopted our exclusive use of winner-take-all, geographically defined single-member districts to elect their national legislatures.

Indeed, it's quite possible that we ourselves wouldn't have chosen the present system if we knew then what we know now. Not many Americans realize that single-member congressional districts are not demanded by the Constitution and weren't required by statute until the 1840s. Senator Charles Buckalew of Pennsylvania was one of the leading proponents of districting, but he later became a leading advocate of proportional representation. In a speech in Philadelphia in 1867, he described why he would have supported PR instead, had he known about it at the time he campaigned to abandon at-large elections:

> What was the idea of [requiring districts]? . . . The idea was to break up the political community, and allow the different political interests which compose it . . . to be represented in the Legislature of the State. Unfortunately, when that arrangement was made . . . this just, equal, almost perfect system of voting [cumulative voting] . . . was unknown; it had not then been announced abroad or considered here, and we did what best we could.

In the nineteenth century, geographic districting made tremendous sense. People's interests—especially to the extent that those interests were relevant to the very limited government of the era—often were primarily defined by where they lived. Transportation and communication were sufficiently rudimentary that political campaigns and voting itself were necessarily based on geography. Today, of course, many citizens' most pressing interests, particularly at the federal level, are not primarily defined by where they live, and we probably would pick a different system if we were starting from scratch.

But of course we're not. Thus, we need to take into account the existing political system and the values and attitudes it has produced when we think about reform. Reforming the election system may be a little bit like squeezing a water balloon: if we press at one end, new difficulties may pop out somewhere else in the system, perhaps somewhere unexpected. Given the tangle of interrelated problems, I'm skeptical that the use of winner-take-all, single-member districts is the principal cause of all our woes or that proportional representation is a magic bullet.

At the federal level, for example, pure forms of PR might be treacherous indeed. Imagine, for example, California electing its 52 U.S. Representatives statewide, or Texas electing its 30, or even Virginia electing its 11. The costs of campaigning effectively would be astronomical, and those costs would likely fall especially heavily on candidates seeking their support from less-wealthy constituencies. PR might exacerbate, rather than cure, the campaign finance problems that plague the current system. The ballot might be so long and confusing that voters would "roll off"—leave the voting booth in frustration without casting a full vote. In addition, some regions of a state—particularly the least economically developed, like Southside Virginia or the border area in Texas—might find that none of the elected representatives lived there; given that people's expectations of representation are at least partially still based on geography, these voters might become more alienated, rather than less. Moreover, although Richie and Hill largely assume that PR benefits progressive causes, I see a substantial danger that far-right and rabid-fringe-left extremists could easily elect candidates if only 2 to 3 percent of the votes cast were sufficient to elect a candidate: it's worth remembering that in 1980, a Grand Dragon of the Ku Klux Klan won the Democratic nomination for a House seat in the San Diego area in a primary with low turnout.

So we need to be more modest in our goals. Richie and Hill themselves implicitly recognize these points when they suggest creating three-member congressional districts. Such districts would essentially require a group to be somewhat more than a quarter of the electorate before it could elect a candidate, and thus may draw an appropriate balance between fairly representing numerical minorities and encouraging voters to build broader coalitions.

Focusing on reforming election structures for local elections—city councils, local school boards, and the like—may be an even more promising tack. Here, the potential problems with PR are far less daunting and the possibility of actually changing the system is far greater, since voter initiatives can require adoption of PR systems without first persuading incumbent legislators to give up the system that got them where they are. Moreover, one of the lessons our history teaches us is that local experimentation often produces national movement. Considering proportional representation may lead us to think more globally—both about the problems of contemporary American politics and about possible alternatives to the current system—but it should probably lead us to act more locally.

3

REPLY

ROBERT RICHIE AND STEVEN HILL

We are pleased that all respondents express willingness to try proportional representation (PR) in the United States. Considering how little time, energy, and thought have been given to PR by U.S. activists and academics in recent decades, this consensus is encouraging. It is no doubt a measure of our broken politics and the powerful logic of PR.

Our respondents are less united on where and how to use PR. This combination of support for the general principle with uncertainty over details invites our recommended strategy of blue-ribbon commissions in states and localities to study which forms of PR might best address problems of declining participation and weak representation.

As to the criticisms of our argument and proposal: Though PR is no panacea, we think that nearly all the questions raised by our respondents have compelling answers. As space constraints prevent us from providing the exhaustive response they deserve, we will here focus on two large questions:

What should the politics of a PR movement look like?
Would the introduction of PR have undesirable unin-
tended consequences?
In answering those questions, we premise two general
points about the nature and importance of PR. First, because PR comes in so many varieties—there are nearly as
many forms of PR as there are nations using it—critics
(and proponents) need to be careful about extrapolating
from the experience of particular forms of PR in particular nations. Second, PR is not a substitute for active political participation by people who care about justice. It
is not the solution to social injustice, but a way to make it
easier for people who care about correcting injustice to
act with greater effect.

POLITICS

Anthony Thigpenn is right: PR will have some fierce opponents. But Thigpenn overlooks potential allies. For
example, as the comments of Cynthia McKinney and
Joshua Rosenkranz indicate, PR systems may be the best
way—both legally and politically—out of current battles over the Voting Rights Act: a way to combat vote dilution and achieve fairness for minorities without rely-
ing on race-conscious districting. With tough-minded
legislators and lawyers like McKinney and Rosenkranz
ready to promote PR (and with harsh critics of traditional winner-take-all remedies like Clarence Thomas

expressing openness to it), the reapportionment after 2000 creates real opportunities for short-term breakthroughs in enacting forms of PR.

As Representative McKinney also points out, some incumbent legislators may appreciate how PR gives them greater control over their electoral destiny. In addition, experience in countries with PR suggests that political elites sometimes recognize that it is better for a city or state to bend toward democracy with PR than to break into turmoil without it. A charter commission in Anthony Thigpenn's city of Los Angeles already is showing serious interest in PR, and one in neighboring Pasadena this year recommended adoption of PR for school board elections.

A similar task force in San Francisco, composed of political insiders, recommended that the choice voting method of PR be placed on the ballot; the resulting campaign in 1996 received a near sweep of endorsements from major political forces in the city, including Mayor Willie Brown and the Democratic Party, and won 44 percent of the vote. With more resources and a longer campaign—supporters had barely three months and $30,000 to reach a city of more than 600,000 adults—PR might have won.

We agree with Thigpenn that the politics of PR will be strengthened by reaching beyond political insiders, and connecting PR to a broader pro-democracy movement. Moreover, as Thigpenn and Ross Mirkarimi suggest, the economic dislocation and environmental damage created by the global economy may provide especially powerful motivators for change. These forces certainly played a primary role in New Zealand in 1993, where voters forced a national referendum on PR and then, despite a massive spending advantage for the opposition, rejected their 140-year-old, American-style system in favor of PR. Still, we expect membership in PR coalitions to vary from place to place.

Finally, Dan Cantor and Pam Karlan correctly observe that local elections provide good opportunities to work for PR. The case for PR is strong in localities, particularly those facing political stagnation due to one-party domination, battles over how to represent increasingly complex diversity, and concerns from wary suburban and urban voters about being shut out by the other side.[1] Local campaigns will definitely help politically: for many Americans, the success of PR in a neighboring town will mean far more than stories about PR in overseas elections.

But we should not settle for a combination of blue-ribbon commissions and local campaigns. If winner-take-all politics is as broken as we believe it to be, then we also need to reform the state and national elections that are most important to most Americans. We hope to see advocates not only working locally, but also promoting instant runoff voting for presidential elections in 2000 and PR for all legislative elections in the redistricting battles of 2001 to 2002. If they emphasize the virtues of PR as an alternative to race-conscious districting, build alliances with sympathetic elected officials, work with other democracy reformers who are taking on campaign finance, entrenched incumbency, and underrepresentation of women and racial minorities, and combine local with national efforts, we think they can achieve important victories.

TROUBLES?

Advocating PR for state and national elections—and thus a real multiparty democracy in the United States—means we need good answers to questions raised by Gary Cox and John Ferejohn. This task is complicated because their central concerns are in direct conflict. Cox argues that PR promotes instability because it increases the chances of divided government. Ferejohn argues that PR promotes excessive stability because substantial electoral shifts may not change the coalition of parties running the government. At the root of their difference is that Cox analyzes presidential democracies, while Ferejohn focuses on parliamentary systems.

The fact that Cox sees possibilities in choice voting in three-seat districts in our presidential system is significant, as this reform would substantially improve our politics. But we think he overstates the dangers in moving further in a proportional direction. Not all comparative political scientists are so cautious: Arend Lijphart and Matthew Shugart both support PR for congressional elections within our current constitutional structure, and we simply don't foresee legislative collapses or Latin American–style instability resulting from more multipartyism in state legislatures.

In any case, Cox's argument about instability really is an indictment of presidentialism, as his comments on irresponsible policy-making within our current electoral system indicate. We believe these policy-making problems are exacerbated by our two-party monopoly. A national Congress elected by an appropriate form of PR—with two broadly representative major parties and three or four smaller parties, for example—would change current "zero sum politics" that lead parties to attack each other rather than conduct the nation's business. As affirmed by observers of cumulative voting in Illinois, representation of more interests can make it easier to break logjams. And given a norm of divided government, the need to have broader political debate and representatives strongly articulating dissenting views is especially important for transforming public opinion and building the necessary consensus for changes in policy.

John Ferejohn raises several skeptical concerns that we believe our article already addressed: about whether PR promotes good governance (we again note Huber and Powell's findings); about whether it boosts voter turnout (which Ferejohn himself suggests later when writing that PR promotes "a politics of mobilization"); and about whether it fosters political accommodation among elected representatives (note our discussion of voting rights and PR's history in American cities).

But Ferejohn's most important critique is that PR undercuts the relationship between electoral expressions of public opinion and policy: that policy remains fixed, despite shifts in opinion. We strongly disagree: the Huber and Powell study, again, is significant in finding that policy in PR democracies more closely mirrors the will of the majority. Moreover, we need to ask about Ferejohn's baseline for comparison: Certainly the many nonvoters in the United States would question Ferejohn's implicit thesis that American politics now promotes electoral responsiveness. As Cox suggests, we have a recurring "grand coalition" between Democrats and Republicans—one that unsurprisingly has become more responsive to well-organized and well-financed corporate interests than to voters who so rarely can cause significant change in control of Congress.

PR, on the other hand, gives voters a realistic chance to vote for new parties or switch their vote among existing parties, if disappointed. Among many nations with PR, the Republic of Ireland provides perhaps the clearest answer to Ferejohn's charge about electoral unresponsiveness. Using choice voting, Irish voters have turned out their incumbent government in every election for over two decades—while also experiencing Europe's highest economic growth rate without British-style slashing of social programs.

We believe Ferejohn's reference to Weimar Germany reflects the undue influence exercised on a generation of American political scientists by former Notre Dame professor Ferdinand Hermens. Hermens's writings played a key role in PR's setbacks in the United States during the cold war, but have been discredited by history. Contemporary German scholars and political leaders dismiss the role of PR in Hitler's rise to power.[2] Germany of course adopted PR after World War II, and its system is widely recognized as a success.

We also believe Ferejohn exaggerates the role of PR in problems in Italy, Israel, and Poland, which all modified their PR systems rather than adopt winner-take-all elections. Every new democracy in eastern Europe freely adopted PR when choosing an electoral system earlier this decade, and most full-fledged democracies use PR for their national elections. Do these democracies succeed despite PR or, as seems more logical, in part because of it? We find Ferejohn's examples atypical, if still important in measuring which specific PR system would suit American politics.

AMERICAN CONTEXT

We conclude by addressing two concerns raised by Pam Karlan that are particularly important to answer in the context of current U.S. politics. First, she suggests that PR elections could compound the problems of campaign finance by increasing the geographic range over which candidates would need to compete. We argue that PR instead minimizes much of the electoral impact of campaign cash. In winner-take-all elections, most money is spent on the relatively few swing voters who don't know their own minds—the votes of the rest of us are rarely bought. As a voting-rights expert, Karlan knows that the key for black voters in electing a candidate is not money or district size, but a district where blacks are a voting majority—thus, underfunded black candidates repeatedly have been elected after the introduction of cumulative voting in southern localities.[3] In European PR elections, Green parties win influential numbers of seats despite generally spending far less money than bigger parties. They can succeed because winners need far fewer votes per square area than in winner-take-all elections, and candidates can campaign as a team, sharing costs and having different candidates pursue particular communities of interest—geographic or otherwise—ready to support them.

Karlan also worries about PR empowering well-organized forces on the right. It might have that effect, but what should we conclude? We stand by the golden rule of representation: give unto others the representation you would have them give you. At the same time, experience of PR around the world suggests ways to fine-tune democracy, finding compromises between the extremes of a 1 percent threshold for representation—as in Israel and Italy before 1994—and the 50 percent threshold we have here.[4] With party-based systems, a German-style threshold of 4 or 5 percent tends to give voters a healthy range of choices across the political spectrum, yet still promote two major parties and exclude potentially disruptive extremists.

In the end, though, we believe that accepting a stacked electoral deck will backfire on supporters of a just society. We have much to gain by trading the incentives to demonize opponents associated with winner-take-all elections for the incentives to build and affirm alliances associated with PR. Like Dan Cantor, we put our confidence in ordinary citizens, fully informed and fully represented, rather than in manipulation of rules for temporary advantage. Once the field is leveled with the help of PR, these citizens are our best guarantees against political failure and our best hope for social justice.

APPENDIX A: A PR GLOSSARY

The terminology of electoral system reform can be confusing: the same systems are often called by different names, in part due to developments in different nations and in part due to tactical decisions by reformers. Here are some of the key terms used in our article.

—*R. R. and S. H.*

List System. In this most widely used form of PR, the voter votes for one party and its list of candidates to represent them. Party lists of candidates can be either "closed" or "open." A closed list means that parties determine the order of their candidates to be elected, often by primary or caucus. An open list allows voters to determine a party's list of candidates by indicating preferences for individual candidates. If a party wins 30 percent of the vote, its candidates win roughly 30 percent of the seats in the legislature, 10 percent of the vote wins roughly 10 percent of seats, and so on. Nationwide lists are used in some countries, but most have regional lists in smaller constituencies. A minimum share of the votes can be required to earn representation; Germany has a 5 percent threshold.

Mixed Member Proportional (MMP). Increasingly popular around the world, this hybrid system elects some seats from single-seat, "winner-take-all" districts and some from party lists. MMP combines geographic representation and proportional representation of ideological interests. Depending on how party lists are allocated, MMP can be fully proportional or semiproportional.

Choice Voting. Also known as "single transferable vote" and "preference voting," choice voting is the most common form of PR in

English-speaking nations. Despite being based on voting for candidates rather than parties, it allows blocs of like-minded voters to win proportional representation. Each voter has one vote, but can rank candidates in order of preference (1, 2, 3, etc.), and ranking additional candidates has no impact on a higher choice candidate's chance to win. Candidates win by reaching a "victory threshold" that is roughly the number of votes divided by the number of seats. If a candidate has too little support among first choices to win, votes for that candidate are transferred to voters' next choices.

Instant Runoff Voting (IRV). Also known as "alternative vote" and "majority preference" voting, IRV is based on the same "transferable vote" mechanism as choice voting, but is a "winner-take-all" system for electing a single candidate such as president, mayor, or governor. Each voter has one vote, but can rank candidates in order of preference (e.g., 1–Nader, 2–Perot, 3–Clinton). The ballot count simulates a series of runoff elections. The candidate with the fewest first-place votes is eliminated, and ballots cast for that candidate are "transferred" to second choices as indicated on voters' ballots. This process of transferring votes continues until one of the candidates has a majority.

Cumulative Voting. A semiproportional system used in some American localities. Voters have as many votes as seats elected in their constituency, and can allocate them however they wish—including giving more than one vote to a particular candidate. Cumulative voting is semiproportional because votes can be "wasted" if a candidate receives more than necessary to win, or if two or more candidates "split" the vote of a particular constituency.

For more thorough discussion of these and other forms of PR, see Matthew Shugart and Rein Taagepera, *Seats and Votes* (New Haven: Yale University Press, 1989); Douglas Amy, *Real Choices, New Voices* (New York: Columbia University Press, 1993); and the Institute for Democracy and Electoral Assistance's *Handbook of Electoral System Design* (available at http://www.int-idea.se).

APPENDIX B: RESOURCES

Books

Behind the Ballot Box: A Citizen's Guide to Voting Systems, by Douglas J. Amy. Westport, CT: Praeger Publishers, 2000.

Lift Every Voice, by Lani Guinier. Simon & Schuster, 1998.

Patterns of Democracy: Government Forms and Performance in Thirty-six Countries, by Arend Lijphart. New Haven: Yale University Press, 1999.

A Right to Representation: Proportional Election Systems for the Twenty-first Century, by Kathleen Barber. Columbus, OH: Ohio State University Press, 2000.

United States Electoral Systems: Their Impact on Women and Minorities, edited by Dr. Wilma Rule and Dr. Joseph Zimmerman. Praeger Publishers, 1992.

International IDEA Handbook of Electoral System Design. A valuable reference on all aspects of the design and administration of election systems. Available from the Institute for Democracy and Electoral Assistance (IDEA) (www.idea.int/).

Dubious Democracy 2000. Center for Voting and Democracy. Statistical and written analysis of U.S. House elections (1982–2000) that shows lack of competition and its historical roots (on the Web at www.fairvote.org).

Congress As America. Center for Voting and Democracy. A comparison of the characteristics of Congress with those of the general population.

Proportional Representation: The Case for a Better Election System. Center for Voting and Democracy. A short, informative introduction to proportional representation by Douglas Amy, author of *Real Choices, New Voices.*

ARTICLES

"If Politics Got Real," by Rob Richie and Steven Hill, *The Nation,* October 16, 2000.

"If a Swing State Cares, It's an Issue," by Michael Lind, *New York Times,* October 1, 2000.

"Give Voters a Bigger Voice," by John B. Anderson and Steven Hill, *New York Daily News,* November 12, 2000.

VIDEOS

Instant Runoff Voting. A short, graphic-based video that clearly explains instant runoff voting (available from the Center for Voting and Democracy).

Choice Voting: State of the Art Democracy. A video with stylish graphics on the choice voting form of PR (available from the Center for Voting and Democracy).

WEB SITES

Center for Voting and Democracy (www.fairvote.org)

Proportional Representation Library (www.mtholyoke.edu/acad/polit/damy/prlib.htm)

Electoral Reform Society (www.electoral-reform.org.uk/)

International Institute for Democracy and Electoral Assistance (IDEA) (www.idea.int). Contains a wealth of information about international elections and election systems.

NOTES

ROBERT RICHIE AND STEVEN HILL / *The Case for Proportional Representation*

1. *Representative Government* (1861).

2. See Robert Harmel, "The Impact of New Parties on Party Systems: Lessons for America from European Multiparty Systems" in *Multiparty Politics in America* (New York: Rowman & Littlefield, 1997).

3. See our 1997 report Monopoly Politics on the Web at http://www.igc.org/cvd/.

4. See John Huber and G. Bingham Powell, "Congruence Between Citizens and Policymakers in Two Visions of Liberal Democracy," *World Politics* (April 1994): 291–326.

5. See Arend Lijphart, "Unequal Participation: Democracy's Unresolved Dilemma," in *American Political Science Review* (March 1997): 1–14.

6. See the Center for Voting and Democracy's report *Dubious Democracy*, 2nd ed. (1996). In 1994, turnout was 42 percent in 87 U.S. House races won by margins of less than 10 percent, 39 percent in 388 races won by margins of 10 to 60 percent, and 29 percent in the 54 races won by margins over 60 percent.

7. See Lani Guinier, *Tyranny of the Majority: Fundamental Fairness in Representative Democracy* (New York: The Free Press, 1994); Joseph Zimmerman and Wilma Rule, *United States Electoral Systems: Their Impact on Women and Minorities* (New York: Praeger, 1992); and the Center for Voting and Democracy's *Voting and Democracy Report* for 1993 and 1995.

8. See Kathleen Barber, *Proportional Representation and Election Reform in Ohio* (Columbus, Ohio: Ohio State University Press, 1995).

9. See Robert Darcy, Susan Welch and Janet Clark, *Women, Elections and Representation* (Lincoln, Nebr.: University of Nebraska Press, 1994).

10. There are variations of mixed member PR systems. Germany and New Zealand have fully proportional mixed systems—in which the party list seats compensate for any distortions in the district seats—but most mixed systems are semiproportional.

11. See David Reynolds, *Democracy Unbound: Progressive Challenges to the Two Party System* (Boston: South End Press, 1997).

Gary W. Cox / *Instability?*

1. See particularly Arend Lijphart, *Democracy in Plural Societies* (New Haven, Conn.: Yale University Press, 1977).

Robert Richie and Steven Hill / *Reply*

1. See "Full Representation: The Future of Proportional Election Systems," *National Civic Review* (spring 1998).

2. See, for example, Gordon Smith, *Democracy in Western Germany* (New York: Holmes and Meier Publishers, 1982). Steve Hill also recently conducted interviews with representatives of the Christian Democratic Party and the Green Party in Germany.

3. See Richard Pildes and Kirsten Donoghue, "Cumulative Voting in the United States," *University of Chicago Legal Forum*, vol. 1995.

4. See *International IDEA Handbook of Electoral System Design*, http://www.int-idea.se.

ABOUT THE CONTRIBUTORS

DANIEL CANTOR is the national organizer of the New Party, which is now active in 10 states.

GARY W. COX is professor of political science at the University of California, San Diego. His latest book, *Making Votes Count*, investigates electoral systems and strategic voting worldwide.

JOHN FEREJOHN is Carolyn S. Munro Professor of Political Science and senior fellow of the Hoover Institution at Stanford University. He is the coauthor of *The Personal Vote: Constituency Service and Electoral Independence.*

LANI GUINIER is professor of law at Harvard University School of Law, and author, most recently, of *Lift Every Voice: Turning a Civil Rights Setback into a New Vision of Social Justice.*

STEVEN HILL is the western regional director of the Center for Voting and Democracy. His articles and commentaries have appeared in dozens of newspapers and magazines, including the *Washington Post, Los Angeles Times, Wall Street Journal, New York Daily News, Chicago Sun-Times, The Nation, Ms., Roll Call, Miami Herald,* and *Baltimore Sun,* and in the anthologies *Making Every Vote Count* and *Civil Rights Since 1787.*

PAMELA S. KARLAN is professor of law and Roy L. and Rosamond Woodruff Morgan Research Professor at the University of Virginia. She is the coauthor of *The Law of Democracy.*

CYNTHIA MCKINNEY is the U.S. Representative from Georgia's Fourth Congressional District. She serves on the House National Security and International Relations Committee.

ROSS MIRKARIMI works for the San Francisco district attorney's Special Prosecutions and Environmental Protection Units. He has directed political campaigns for both electoral reform and progressive candidates, including Terence Hallinan's successful campaign for district attorney.

ROBERT RICHIE is executive director of the Center for Voting and Democracy, a nonprofit, nonpartisan organization that advocates electoral reforms to increase voter participation and provide fair representation. His writings have appeared in several publications and anthologies. Before cofounding the Center, Richie worked as a political consultant on three winning congressional campaigns in Washington state and as a media relations specialist for nonprofit organizations.

E. JOSHUA ROSENKRANZ is executive director of the Brennan Center for Justice at NYU Law School. The Center is engaged in scholarship and action on issues of democracy and other areas.

ANTHONY THIGPENN chairs the board of Agenda, a community-based organization in South Los Angeles, and is one of the founders of the Los Angeles Metropolitan Alliance.